Praise for *Tommy*, Trauma, and Postwar Youth Culture

"Few albums have undergone the intense scrutiny of the Who's *Tommy*, which may prompt skeptics to argue against the need for another analysis of this complex, seminal rock opera. Such an attitude, however, would mean overlooking Dewar MacLeod's fascinating study. In his nuanced, compelling, and comprehensive examination of a work that remains both profound and obscure, MacLeod artfully charts Pete Townshend's artistic progression as he single-handedly brings the Who from Mod-era pop stardom into a rapidly expanding creative universe that, in *Tommy*, articulates his desire for transcendence and deep, eternal peace. MacLeod situates the pre-history of *Tommy* in the youth culture of post-War England and examines the profound effect of trauma on Tommy and how his attendant disabilities form a shield offering protection from a forcefully intruding, violent, and abusive external environment. What MacLeod is asking of us is to reconsider Tommy as victim and, latterly, messiah, and the record in its entirety as a more arcane and multilayered consideration of search for spiritual tranquility during a tumultuous time in cultural history. And, in doing so, provides us with a fresh perspective on an enduring and significant moment in rock history."

— John Dougan, Professor of Popular Music Studies,
Middle Tennessee State University,
and author of *The Who Sell Out*

"Passionately written, this book expertly and perceptively connects the first rock opera to Pete Townshend's quest to understand his troubling childhood abuse."

— David Szatmary, author of *Rockin' in Time, 6th edition*

"Dewar MacLeod's reflection on the Who's classic album *Tommy* offers a masterclass in bringing historical meaning to popular music. His examination takes Townshend's work, embedding it in time and space, while drawing out greater historical and cultural meaning for the reader. MacLeod also reveals the uncomfortable locale of rock music—a mass produced product infused with deeper artistic depth, straddling the supposedly firm divide between art and product. While never settling the question, he gives us a deeper understanding of the production of culture in the age of its mass reproduction. This book is a timely reminder that culture is most productively understood when placed with its larger historical context."

— Mindy Clegg, author of *Punk Rock: Music Is the Currency of Life*

Tommy, Trauma, and Postwar Youth Culture

Tommy, Trauma, and Postwar Youth Culture

Dewar MacLeod

EXCELSIOR
EDITIONS

Color photo of Roger Daltrey with arm raised holding microphone at Woodstock, 1969 (cropped). Used by permission of Henry Diltz.

Published by State University of New York Press, Albany

© 2023 State University of New York

Printed in the United States of America

Excelsior Editions is an imprint of State University of New York Press

For information, contact State University of New York Press, Albany, NY www.sunypress.edu

Library of Congress Cataloging-in-Publication Data

Name: MacLeod, Dewar, 1962– author.
Title: Tommy, trauma, and postwar youth culture / Dewar MacLeod.
Description: Albany : State University of New York Press, 2023. | Series: Excelsior Editions | Includes bibliographical references and index.
Identifiers: LCCN 2022022749 | ISBN 9781438491745 (pbk. : alk. paper) | ISBN 9781438491752 (ebook)
Subjects: LCSH: Townshend, Pete. | Who (Musical group). Tommy. | Townshend, Pete. Tommy (Opera) | Townshend, Pete. Tommy (Opera) (Libretto) | Townshend, Pete. Who's Tommy. | Rock music— Psychological aspects.
Classification: LCC ML410.T69 M33 2023 | DDC 782.42166092—dc23/ eng/20220518
LC record available at https://lccn.loc.gov/2022022749

10 9 8 7 6 5 4 3 2 1

For Jackie, Sheila, and Jennifer

Contents

Acknowledgments

At William Paterson University, I am grateful for able research help from Stephen Pellegrini, the interlibrary loan crew at Cheng Library, and librarian extraordinaire Richard Kearney. This project was supported also by Assigned Research Time and a timely sabbatical. The History Department's best asset, Malissa Williams, helped me through countless problems little and big along the way.

For first encouraging me to undertake this project many, many years ago (I'm sure he doesn't even remember), thanks to Stuart Ewen. I am ever grateful to those who most influenced my thinking as a historian: Berta Bilezikjian, D. Carroll Joynes, Carol Berkin, and David Nasaw. For helpful comments and encouragement during the writing process, thanks to Rory MacLeod, Sinéad MacLeod, Sharon Freedman, David McBride, Doug Hill, David Schiller, Roger Sedarat, Dionne Ford, Kevin Delaney, Timothy J. Smith, and Maureen Blandino. Thanks to colleagues at the 2019 *Balancing the Mix* Conference in Memphis, where I presented my first public thoughts on this project, and to Kathy Curto and the members of her wonderful writing workshop for helping me sharpen my voice. The folks who curate the collections at thewho. net made my research job a great deal easier.

A few years ago I was fortunate to cross paths with Richard Carlin. He has been a tremendously supportive editor at SUNY Press, where I have had a smooth and joyful experience (so far!)

bringing this book to print. Thanks to Alicia Brady, Michael Campochiaro, Susan Geraghty, Laura Tendler, and Aimee Harrison for her beautiful cover. For the cover, I am grateful to the legendary Henry Diltz for the glorious image from Woodstock and to his archivist Gary Strobl for making it happen.

Thanks to Nicola Joss for responding respectfully to my initial query and to Pete Townshend for answering swiftly and honestly and directly.

Finally, my deepest gratitude to my friends Joel Naftelberg and Christine Kelly for years of love and friendship and for showing me how to face life and death with grace, dignity, and joy.

Introduction

"I want nothing to do with it"

It stung a bit to be rejected by Pete Townshend, I admit. His tone comes through a little clipped, a bit snippy, maybe freighted with judgment . . .

But can you blame him? I was asking him to revisit something he himself has been wrestling with his whole life, which led him to create a lasting work of art and continue to re-create new versions of it throughout his career, as audiences clamored, as other artists dreamed of collaborating, as the story continued to resonate, to reveal new possibilities, to break and uplift hearts.

It feels cheap, low, dirty to rat out Pete Townshend when he had the good graces to respond to me. His email was not "off the record," but he sent it to me personally (through his longtime trusted assistant Nicola). He didn't have do to that. She didn't have to do that. I had sent a request, with an attached one-page proposal, and they responded within a few days! Nicola replied that Pete was on sabbatical, taking a yearlong break from music-related activities, and he would not be available for an interview. And that was that, or so I thought. The next day she forwarded me his thoughts and his personal reason for not wanting to go into it.

> Sabbatical aside, I really don't think there is anything I can add to what I've said over the years about Tommy,

1

but there is another issue, which is that of his pitch to . . . [as I had written to him:] "But, more importantly, I would like delve into the personal aspects of the story—in particular, the relationships between abuse, trauma, addiction, recovery, and spirituality as they are expressed in *Tommy*."

And that, he said, ". . . is definitely off-limits for me now."

Pete closed with, "So thank him for his engagement, and wish him the best of luck, but I want nothing to do with it."

Ouch.

But can you blame him? I was asking him to revisit his work on terms that were most deep, raw, and personal.

He did not have to write anything. He did not even have to respond. And, then, when he read my proposal, he did so carefully, thoughtfully, generously even, as he clipped the part that stood out. This chapter should be titled "My encounter with the thoughtful and generous Pete Townshend, who took the time to respond to my query when he really, really didn't have to."

It's tough to actually "cherish" an email. Not much of an item to really hold on to. No physicality in the digital age. Sure, the font is different—WebKit-standard, I am told by my Microsoft Office software—with a slight bluish tint. His words are set off, helpfully indented by Nicola. But I can hardly snuggle up to those words, rub them against my cheek, whisper conspiratorially, breathe deeply of their essence, carry them around and show them to any and all who might care. It's hardly a locket with a heart-shaped photo or a lock of Pete's hair.

But I cherish the email nonetheless, as it is proof that I did indeed reach out, that I have finally begun my exploration into the first album I ever bought, with the story that defined my life. I am not a journalist, used to doors closed in my face and phones slammed down into receivers as I doggedly pursue the truth, overcoming all obstacles and resistance. I became a historian so that I could avoid interactions with people.

". . . but I want nothing to do with it."

How dare you? he seems to say to me. This is exactly the problem I am wrestling with, which I finally overcome for a brief moment, just enough to have the courage to reach out, speak out, after a lifetime of silence, fifty-plus years of retreat into a state of disengagement with the world. I wasn't quite Tommy, but I certainly recognized a kindred spirit.

Being rejected for an interview is hardly a hook to hang a book on, but when it is the one person who can evoke the "how dare you" feeling more than any other, the very same person who wrote the words that defined my life as I was living it—"You didn't hear it / You didn't see it"—whose voice commanded—"You won't say nothing to no-one / Never tell a soul / What you know is the Truth"—it's enough to get started.

Chapter 1

The Plot

Tommy takes us on an inner journey, the inner journey of a generation. The story, briefly:

Tommy is born into war. Captain Walker returns, years after the war, to find his wife in the arms of another man; he kills the man, an act witnessed (reflected in a mirror) by their young son Tommy. "What about the boy?" Captain and Mrs. Walker ask each other, "He saw it all!"

They solve the problem by instructing the boy to forget what he saw: "You didn't hear it. You didn't see it. You won't say nothing to no one, never tell a soul what you know is the truth."

Tommy is silenced, becoming a "deaf, dumb and blind boy," traumatized into a kind of dissociative, autistic state. But distantly, as if already in another dimension, we hear (barely) the boy's response: ("I heard it"; "I saw it"; "I won't say nothing to no one"; "Never tell a soul what I know is the truth").

The first half of the album takes us through Tommy's "Amazing Journey" both inner and outer, and the parallel attempts of his parents to find a cure for his deaf, dumb, and blind condition, while also leaving him to be subjected to abuse by his cousin and uncle. Cut off from the world, Tommy goes deeper and deeper into his self, capable only of staring at himself in the mirror, the sole place where he seems to experience any life-force. Tommy's incantation of "See me, feel me, touch me, heal me" calls out of the darkness as a personal plea of desperation.

Oh, and somewhere along the way, he becomes a pinball champion.

Eventually, Tommy's mother grows so frustrated she smashes the mirror that he stares into all day, shattering his world of illusion and launching him into the world of reality. He is cured and becomes a social phenomenon, a celebrity, a rock star, to some the new messiah.

Tommy experiences the breakthrough as a deeply spiritual moment, suffused with beauty and perfection, what Pete calls "god-realised," his inner realm of pure light and revelation, the primal self, with illusion stripped away, connected with all humanity and all the universe. Tommy becomes fully free by simply letting go of illusion and embracing reality. He almost can't believe it, and he senses neither will his new audience: "You'd laugh and say nothing's that simple."

Tommy rather innocently wants to invite all of his followers to join him, opening his house, and then building a greater and greater house to accommodate all who want liberation and transcendence. Tommy wants them all simply to be true to themselves, but they demand a leader who will tell them what to do.

The masses embrace him, and a utopian vision beckons, but both he and they rebel against the constraints and possibilities. He starts to issue edicts, but only to force them to look inward. Uncle Ernie—previously his molester—takes over the business and becomes a hustler and conman, turning the whole enterprise into a swindle for the benighted, desperate-to-be-brainwashed mob.

The whole thing comes crashing down, as the followers rebel against Tommy, chanting "We're Not Gonna Take It" in the final song, as Tommy's "See me, feel me, touch me, heal me" remains unfulfilled, with a rousing chorus taking us to the fade out, "Listening to you, I get the music, gazing at you, I get the heat . . ."

It really is a brilliant composition. As a musical piece, it feels full, complete. What a deliverance from "Overture" to the anthem at the end. There is a complete story there, and we have been taken through it with confidence. The song cycle feels so fulfilling. The band is in command throughout, with the propulsive rhythm section of Keith Moon and John Entwistle powering us forward, and the vocals of Roger Daltrey and Pete moving and evocative.

The story is upsetting, even harrowing. It doesn't always add up, and at times is barely comprehensible. And I'm not sure I feel delivered, even at the end in terms of where Tommy is. Has Tommy been saved? Have we? There is still a darkness, a wariness. Is cynicism too strong a word? What is Tommy's perspective on his past? Does he forgive? Does he remember? What is guiding him? What fuels him to do what he does? He is a guru who has found the key to enlightenment. But what is that? What does he want his followers to do? And to what end? What is he/they not gonna take? We are not gonna let the elders who abused us do so anymore? And we are not gonna repeat what they have done with their organized religion and attempts at manipulation of the people?

After he is healed, Tommy becomes a spiritual guru, and the album's story serves as a cautionary tale about the dangers of idolatry and hero worship and a retreat from pursuit of social change. The album emerged as a statement of youth movement at a pivotal moment—the same year as Woodstock, Altamont, and the Manson family murders. *Tommy* simultaneously chronicles, enacts, and rejects the pursuit of any larger vision of social justice in the counterculture as the 1960s drew to a close.

Chapter 2

"California, Here I Come"

Still the most powerful and nostalgic memory of my life is the train trip my family and I took across the country in the summer of 1969. I suppose we were like so many immigrants sold on the American story, out to make a better life. My father was a World War II vet of the Royal Canadian Air Force, a bombardier on a Lancaster airplane. His war stories could not be pried out of him, except for the loss of his beloved and revered older brother, a Mosquito pilot shot down over Belgium in 1944. After the war, college, and medical school on his veteran's benefits, he found a suitable woman to build a family with in Nova Scotia, in the little city of Halifax and the tiny seaside town of Liverpool, an hour down the coast. Raising five kids (with another lost soon after childbirth), they somehow got it in their minds to go for more.

So, late in 1968, we moved out of our house on Rosebank Avenue in Halifax into an apartment in Embassy Towers for an eventual move to California. We spent the rest of the school year being driven to school by a taxi driver named Earl, singing "California here I come, right back where I started from." I remember the excitement of sitting on boxes for days watching on our little

9

black-and-white television the coverage of the American flight to the moon and the landing on July 20, 1969.

My father liked to tell the story that he asked his friends for advice on how best to move this large brood of five kids (aged five to twelve) across the continent to Los Angeles. They all told him to just get on the plane and get it over with as fast as possible. Instead, we loaded all our stuff into giant moving vans and boarded the cross-country train in August 1969. I turned seven on the trip, and I remember viscerally my wonder and joy at the freedom I felt traveling on the train. Those were the days when parents could neglect their kids without violating any social norms, so I was free to roam the train as I saw fit. I suppose my parents probably did know where I was and what I was doing, but their presence is almost absent from my memories of the journey, other than during the transfer at Chicago's great Union Station, where we huddled around our assembled belongings waiting for the next leg.

The whole thing couldn't have taken more than a few days, but it felt like it stretched out forever. I followed the porters as they made their rounds, making the beds and folding them back up into the walls. I got a watch for my seventh birthday on the train, and I would roam back and forth up and down the train so that people could ask me what time it is. I would answer, "Right here it is noon, in LA it is 10:00 a.m., and in Nova Scotia it is 2:00 p.m." I was, briefly, a precocious child.

We were greeted at Union Station in Los Angeles by two cars, one a shiny, broad convertible. I was placed in the middle of the front seat—without a seat belt, of course—and was treated to that scene that was a cliché of LA driving scenes in movies, but was my real introduction. Head tilted back, I watched the sun-drenched Southern California sky glide by through a palm tree canopy. California, here I come, indeed.

We arrived in Los Angeles as yokels, checking into a motel on the Sunset Strip with a kidney-shaped pool. We moved into a house on Highland Avenue before our possessions arrived, and a month later moved into another house in a different neighborhood, my parents having seen fit to move to another country and across a continent without properly vetting the school districts. We made the journey across the country while the Woodstock music festival was taking place and arrived in Los Angeles within days of the Manson family murders.

My earliest memories are music, of my rocking back and forth on my knees to the singles in our family collection—curated by my older brother—Malvina Reynold's "Little Boxes," "This Land Is Your Land" (the Canadian version—"From Bonavista to Vancouver Island"), and the Beatles' "She Loves You" and "I Want To Hold Your Hand." When we arrived in LA we quickly discovered KHJ's "Boss Radio" ("KHJ plays all the hits!"), and I listened day and night to all the DJs: Charlie Tuna, The Real Don Steele, Humble Harv, Robert W. Morgan.

The first album I bought with my own money was *Tommy* from the Wherehouse Record store in Westwood, the college town for UCLA. My brother would take me on trips, for him to visit the headshops and what seemed like exotic emporiums but were more likely touristy places, where he shopped for posters of Jimi Hendrix and used blue jeans.

My connection to *Tommy* is oblique. I was seven years old when I first heard and instantly immersed myself in it. But this album was not meant for me. It was meant for those, like Tommy, who had been through rough childhoods and were now delivering themselves through the church of rock 'n' roll, worshipping alone, in groups, and especially in cathedrals like the Fillmore East. It was meant for those boomers who were part of "My Generation." I was born at the tail end of that baby boom, still statistically lumped into the cohort, but very much out of the cultural moment of the Woodstock Nation.

I remember exactly where we were when my brother told me that *Tommy* was a true story, that he was Keith Moon's brother. I

believed him because my brother was my Cousin Kevin and my
Uncle Ernie. I wasn't living the deliverance of Tommy that comes
at the end of the record. I was still living side one.

Chapter 3

Historical Background

"It's a boy, Mr. Townshend"

Tommy was born into war, and so were the Who, all of them born between 1944 and 1946. Their mothers gave birth in the waning days and early aftermath of a national and global trauma. Roger was born during the "baby blitz" of 1944, that last, desperate German air offensive of the war. Pete claimed, "I was born in the hour that Albert Speer was arrested. . . . My father got these two messages: Speer's been captured, and the other 'It's a boy, Mr. Townshend' "—providing the opening words for *Tommy*.[1] The members of the Who, and their audience, grew up under the shadow of the war and its long aftermath, their world now defined both by the steady decline of England's mastery of the globe *and* rising affluence, with more time and money for young people coming of age. The war was over, and a new world was being born.

There was certainly in Britain a shared experience of being born during or immediately after the war. "[A]ll the war babies, all the old soldiers coming back from war and screwing until

13

they were blue in the face—this was the result," according to Pete. "Thousands and thousands of kids, too many kids, not enough teachers, not enough parents . . ."[2]

The nation and the continent of Europe teetered on the brink of all-out chaos for the first few years of those babies' lives. Rationing continued in England while starvation swept the continent during the brutal winters. The members of the Who and their audience grew up under the shadow of the war and its long aftermath. To be born in 1944 or 1946 in London, or even the small towns of the English countryside, was to come into a world with visible reminders of the devastation, death, and loss; of rubble and rationing. This recent history connected to a much longer history of the British experience in the world.

It's as if the trauma was epigenetic for the youth of the postwar era, their parents also born into war: to a generation whose young men had disappeared in the First World War, their bodies lying "in Flanders fields [where] poppies blow/Between the crosses, row on row." Their parents' own childhoods defined by recovery from the devastation of the Great War and then the Great Depression, they were thrust as teenagers and young adults into the Second World War. Their own trauma shaping their identities, they were now raising children with, one can imagine, severely constricted emotional capacities.

Despite achieving their "Finest Hour"—epitomized in Churchill's post-Dunkirk speech "we shall fight on the beaches . . . we shall never surrender"—the famous British stiff upper lip had been put severely to the test.[3] And even with victory in 1945, it was not over.

The British had ruled the globe but at home retained much of the sheltered vision of an isolated island nation. It was a bleak, dark, twisted world, the narrow, cloistered, provincial world of suspicion and superstition, a world of the village and the family that contained and constrained. The closed-minded village elders who know what is good for you, and charlatans and hucksters who glide through to prey upon the weak and the desperate. This is the world of British history coming of age in the aftermath of the war. Despite all its pretentions to civilization and supremacy, there still was something almost medieval about the British worldview. It could still be a tiny island of narrow limits, with no place for difference or dissent. It still was too often ruled by idiots and bullies.

But what came with victory was the steady decline of England's mastery of the globe, the slow-motion disintegration of the British Empire as India, Malaya, Egypt, and a succession of colonies across the world peeled themselves off from the yoke of "civilization." Churchill's "Empire beyond the seas, armed and guarded by the British Fleet," could no longer "carry on the struggle," and gradually, reluctantly, the country's leaders came to accept that Britannia no longer ruled the waves, and a new Britain would need to be born.[4]

The first years of austerity gradually created a political consensus promoting a welfare state and near-full employment slowly leading to postwar recovery and rising expectations. For Pete, this meant a world of opportunity held back by fearful adults: "For the first time in history a whole generation had the economic and educational opportunity to turn their backs on the dead-end factory jobs of their parents, who, traumatized by two world wars, had responded by creating a safety blanket of conformity."[5]

For the first time in generations, the leaders of society had to confront the problem that their young men were no longer dying. What to do with all these young people coming of age? What does a society do with an excess of young people, just as the adults are trying to crawl out of the wreckage and re-create a stable society—even if they were half-deluded that the good old days could be brought back? You apprentice some to the trades; you send the best and brightest (and richest) to the universities; and you park the potential misfits into art schools, where they can all meet and make up their own world together.

Young people came of age in an environment of mixed messages and sentiments. Prime Minister Harold Macmillan's famous 1957 speech announcing that "most of our people have never had it so good" may have been true, but it was a long time coming, ignoring the difficult childhoods of these war babies. Even with more spending money and free time, young people still felt frustration, resentment, and anger at the constraints of British society.[6]

And then something crazy and inexplicable happened. Something similar had begun a bit earlier in the United States when rock 'n' roll emerged in the mid-1950s. In the early 1960s, this postwar generation of British youth rewrote the whole story. "Europe is a piss place for music and it's a complete incredible fluke that England ever got it together," Townshend noted in 1968. "And just all of a sudden, bang! wack! zap-swock out of nowhere. There it is: the Beatles. Incredible. How did they ever appear then on the poxy little shit-stained island."[7]

Suddenly, it seemed, young people could glimpse a future they were in the process of making, but only dimly, as if emerging from a black-and-white world into a colorful one (in fact, the Beatles' first film was still in black-and-white). Pete, Roger, John, and Keith came together in 1964 as the Who and quickly rose in the Beatles' wake—alongside the Rolling Stones, the Kinks, and hundreds of other bands.

The Who emerged as young men themselves with an audience of "teenagers" that was trans-Atlantic and increasingly global.[8] Never before had the cultural, technological, and political environments allowed for such rapid and widespread diffusion of culture, with young people often in the lead. "In this surge of hope and optimism," Pete claims, "The Who set out to articulate the joy and rage of a generation struggling for life and freedom."[9]

The Who found their identity in alignment with the Mod subculture, "an army, a powerful, aggressive army of teenagers with transport."[10] While the Mods presented the band with an image, a way of distinguishing themselves from other groups, the movement also expressed Townshend's emerging perception of himself as an artist and performer. Pete had attended Ealing Art College, and from the start he sought to integrate his art-school training of mixing pop with avant-garde sensibilities.

The Mods offered him as well a way of seeing himself as part of something larger, as having social, maybe even historical, impact. "You see, as individuals these people were nothing. They were the lowest, they were England's lowest common denominators," Pete explained to an American rock journalist in 1968. "Not only were they young, they were also lower class young. They had to submit to the middle classes' way of dressing and way of speaking and way of acting in order to get the very jobs which kept them alive. They had to do everything in terms of what existed already around them."[11]

The Mods mimicked the conformity they were supposed to demonstrate, fetishizing the signifiers of propriety, prosperity, and progress, amplifying the Protestant work ethic by taking speed to be "more productive." Pete admired how they didn't outwardly reject and disobey, but twisted, derailed, mutated the conventional and expected in their dress and behavior: "It made the whole gesture so much more vital. It was incredible. As a force, they were unbelievable."[12]

And it was this "force" that Pete felt, a two-way relationship, a sense of fulfillment by being part of something larger, "that incredible feeling of being part of something which is really something much bigger. . . . It covered everybody, everybody looked the same, and everybody acted the same and everybody wanted to be the same." As Pete described it in 1968, "It was the first move that I have ever seen in the history of youth towards unity, towards unity of thought, unity of drive and unity of motive."[13] From this sensibility, this "transcendence"[14] and drive for unity, Pete wrote his first hits.

With an opening riff baldly stolen from the Kinks, "I Can't Explain" (1964) taught him how to understand and respect his audience, his peers. While he thought he had written a "love song of frustration . . . these uneducated, inarticulate kids" told him "it was actually a song about their inability to communicate their inability to communicate," Townshend discovered. "Now that's a pretty high concept. They got it, and I didn't."[15] Pete considered that his Mod audience "commissioned" him to write the song and then explained to him what it meant: "They asked me how I could have known how they felt and what they had experienced. How could I have explained what they could not explain, that they could not explain anything at all?"[16] From this interaction, Pete gained a key early insight into how he would work as an artist and pop star, and his relationship with this audience became a key thread to his ongoing work: "What the Mods taught us in the band was how to lead by following."[17]

The Who became larger than "a cult within a cult" with the release of "My Generation" in 1965, a song instantly iconic for its brashness ("Hope I die before I get old"), expressing the frustration and ecstasy of youth.[18] The famous stutter ("My-my-my G-g-g-generation") captures perfectly what Greg Shaw, writing in *Crawdaddy*, described as the essence of all the early Who songs: "finding self-image through the release of frustration-born tension. Tension and its release was the whole essence of the Who, both thematically and musically."[19] The stutter serves as a signifier of the tension/release, with the hard consonant hold-ing, holding, holding—like a winch being ratcheted tighter and tighter—until the release bursts forth, spitting out the word and the concept of rebellion against all who hold us back.[20] Who biographer Dave Marsh, who tends toward the hyperbolic in his fandom, claims the song had an "authentically revolutionary" impact as "the Who were the first to apply to everyday pop the principle articulated by John Cage, that music is nothing more than consciously organized noise."[21] Townshend claimed the Who "were leading a revolt against the old values and order of music. Everybody was full of resentment."[22] "My Generation" indelibly stamped them, and songwriter/guitarist Townshend specifically, as a key voice of the rising generation, what was soon to be seen as the counterculture—though they were perhaps more renowned for smashing their instruments. This "auto-destruction" was both a consciously contrived attention-getter and an act of theoretically-based performance art. During his time at Ealing Art College, Pete had first encountered Gustav Metzger's teachings— "Auto-destructive art re-enacts the obsession with destruction, the pummeling to which individuals and masses are subjected."[23] Pete transferred the process of decay and pummeling onto the stage, sped up for the concert timetable, when "you are suddenly faced with what is really happening—the end of the show. A few seconds of total abandon. It seems like a logical end to the way I play, because . . . well, I guess I'll never be able to play the way I want to play."[24]

Chapter 4

1967

Toward the Rock Opera

The year 1967 is when what we think of as "the sixties" really starts to take off. Enough is already happening in the Haight-Ashbury in the Spring—before the Summer of Love—to draw journalist Joan Didion to San Francisco for an immersion by the outsider/citizen-anthropologist to embed with the natives, studying the primates like Joan Goodall in the Gombe National Park, observing, interacting peripherally, careful not to disturb the field of study too much by her actions. And what she finds already is a refuge of the abandoned, an island of spoiled, clueless, unsympathetic, mindless, teen runaways who conform to all the worst fears and hatreds of their middle-American parents.

Didion published a devastating piece in the *Saturday Evening Post* just as the summer was coming to an end. What she finds is a "real social crisis" beyond the already notorious drug use. This is what happens in all romantic movements that start as a "return to innocence" but also as an "itch for the transcendental, for purification," that seeks a leader to drive it toward authoritarianism. Her critique was all the more staggering for her stark, deadpan tone:

> We were seeing the desperate attempt of a handful of pathetically unequipped children to create a community in a social vacuum. . . . This was not a traditional generational rebellion. At some point between 1945 and 1967 we had somehow neglected to tell these children the rules of the game we happened to be playing. Maybe we had stopped believing in the rules ourselves, maybe we were having a failure of nerve about the game. Maybe there were just too few people around to do the telling. These were children who grew up cut loose from the web of cousins and great-aunts and family doctors and lifelong neighbors who had traditionally suggested and enforced society's values.[1]

When we get to the end of the essay, with those young people now parenting kids, dosing them with acid on a daily basis, it is impossible not to believe that, as she says, the world is spinning, spinning, spinning, and the center cannot hold, the centrifugal force will spray us all with the chaos and destruction wreaked by the offal of civilization.

It's terrifying and, because of Didion's unparalleled skill, absolutely cements an image in your mind. But it's also a vicious hit piece, ignoring why youth culture was becoming the counterculture, why pot and acid were becoming central to the hippie experience. It's a strange reading of recent history, as it's hard to believe that young people had not been taught the rules of the game. In fact, Didion ignores how the youth counterculture was very explicit about the reasons for rejecting "the web" that "traditionally suggested and enforced society's values." The stakes seemed higher, within both rock 'n' roll and the wider world. Didion misses how music was no longer a pop sideshow ritual of rebellion and indulgence, but the central creative element of global culture.[2]

The whole generation of musicians was revealing that rock music was more than simple pop songs. The Beatles were no longer singing "She loves you yeah yeah yeah" and "I wanna hold your haaaand." Rock 'n' roll became Rock in the mid-1960s, and it wasn't clear where the Who fit in. Pete had written great rock songs like "I Can't Explain," "Anyway, Anyhow," "Substitute," and "My Generation"—but also "Pictures of Lily," "Happy Jack," "Magic Bus," enjoyable pop craftsmanship, but weird little numbers that verged on novelty songs. But things were getting serious, and no one knew if Pete was up to it. By 1966, with the Beatles' *Revolver*, the Beach Boys' *Pet Sounds*, and Bob Dylan's electric albums, rockers were inspired to do more. By 1967, with *Sgt. Pepper*, with its complex suite of songs, sounds, and lyrics, all pop musicians were put on notice—you are either a pop manufacturer or an artist: take a side.

Pete was the one who wanted to straddle that divide. The rock star is an entertainer, and Pete loved making hits. He wanted to write pop masterpieces that go to the top of the charts as evidence of his brilliance, but also as affirmation of his status. He was an unabashed commercially oriented maker of product for the marketplace. The rock star is also an artist, and Pete saw himself as a Pop Artist, commenting on the whole process of manufacturing hits and stars. *The Who Sell Out* (1967) packaged the band's songs wrapped in mock advertising and jingles, sending up the process, mocking it gently without quite rejecting it. The album's visuals most obviously reference Andy Warhol's Campbell Soup paintings. It is a canny admission and boast as well as self-criticism about where the Who were at the time.

The rock star was also something else, not exactly necessarily a representative or spokesman, but enjoying a new role and relationship with a new type of audience, the rock audience being a bit different from the pop one. Rock stars took different paths, and some rejected the new role outright, but Pete took it head-on. He never wanted to leave the pop song behind, but he also had more complex story and musical ideas to explore for creative, spiritual, and commercial considerations. The Who's co-manager Kit Lambert introduced Pete to opera, encouraging him to expand his vision.[3] In 1966, in search of ways to tell more complex stories, Pete wrote the mini-opera "A Quick One, While He's Away." Musically, the six-part suite—what Pete later called "*Tommy*'s parents"[4]—attempts a more ambitious project than Pete had ever done, combining the best and worst of the Who. The music is classic driven Who, propelled by Keith's vicious drumming, interspersed with silly little ditties and some typical Who juvenile humor (chanting "cello, cello, cello" because they couldn't afford to record a string section).

Thematically, the story is clearly an early stab at the motifs of *Tommy*: the abandoned child, the creepy "seducer" who rapes a child in her Girl Guide uniform, and the insistent forgiveness of the neglecter (and even the abuser?). Depending on your taste, it can seem childish, trivial, or hardly sophisticated, although musically more complex and interesting.

The plot feels curdled and embarrassing in retrospect, and in his autobiography Pete does an interesting job trying to interpret retrospectively what it was all about. He concludes, "Then suddenly, everyone is 'forgiven,' not once but a thousand times, over and over—as though there's not enough forgiveness in a single line. When I sang this part live on stage, I would often become furious, thrashing at my guitar until I could thrash no more, frantically forgiving my mother, her lover, my grandmother, her lovers, and most of all myself."[5] We will see this compulsive attempt to bestow unearned forgiveness return throughout the life of *Tommy*.

Pete's excitement about the possibilities of telling more complex stories while still embracing the pop form sticks out in his interviews at the time. In March 1967, he revealed to the British fan magazine *Beat Instrumental* that he was working on a rock opera, but it is one that his fans would never hear. He's writing it for himself, just trying to see if he can do it. By November 1967, Pete has returned to those fans to reveal that, yes, it is done. The opera has come and gone. He's shown to himself he can do it and has ditched the whole thing. Pete has experimented in the lab with the opera, pronouncing the experiment a success. He then drops on the world a couple of mini-operas, providing proof of concept. And now he is ready to tackle the whole thing.

In fact, a mini-opera shows up on *The Who Sell Out*, a concept album of songs separated by satirical radio commercials. "Rael 1 & 2" was set in 1999 when the "Redchins" (Red Chinese) ruled the world. The futuristic plot reflects Pete's current obsession with UFOs, but the story is never fully developed. Pete intended it to be political, but, as he acknowledged, "I'm not a great political head."[6] Envisioned as a grand suite of songs, it was cut down to fit the needs of the new album. Even Pete concluded, "No-one will ever know what it means, it has been squeezed up too tightly to make sense."[7] The result was an interesting but slight bit of potted psychedelia that doesn't touch Pink Floyd's *Piper at the Gates of Dawn* (1967) or even the Amboy Dukes' "Journey to the Center of Your Mind" (1968)[8]—at least to my mind.

The album also contained their new single "I Can See for Miles," of which Dave Marsh has a wonderfully unobjective take:

> "My Generation" is Townsend's greatest anthemic rock statement, but "I Can See for Miles" is quite simply the most exciting piece of music the Who ever recorded and, by a wide margin, their most effective recording. Its ambition is virtually limitless, and everything it seeks is achieved. Like so much of the Who's music, it is built around drones and crescendos, Townshend's

guitar figure circling Moon cymbal splashes. It starts
out full bore, with a pulsating E chord, sustained
beyond belief, then punctuated with a clattering shot
by Moon. The effect is ominous and hallucinatory."[9]

Marsh is spot on. It was this song, played on AM radio, that
prepared me for *Tommy*: the drone, the hum, the mysterious
mood . . . it all seduced me as I rocked on my hands and knees.

The Who didn't break through in the United States until
their appearance at Monterey in 1967 on their first brief US tour
to support their new album and singles "Happy Jack" and "Pictures of Lily." Staged at the beginning of the Summer of Love just
down the coast from San Francisco, the Monterey International
Pop Festival was the first major rock festival—modeled on the
successful jazz festivals of the time—and featured three days of
rock 'n' roll. With the roster mostly composed of bands from the
rival Los Angeles and San Francisco scenes, the festival wallowed
in hippie vibes—hardly the Who's style. "The Who and their fans,"
one critic writes, "if not openly confrontational toward hippies,
could come across as dismissive."[10] Pete expressed his skepticism
about the whole "love philosophy": "Love is an aggressive and
possessive thing."[11]

It was the first chance that many people in the States had
to see the Who, along with Janis Joplin and Jimi Hendrix, and
all three gave breakthrough, even stunning, performances. If you
want some visceral proof, see D. A. Pennebaker's *Monterey Pop*
(1968), where the camera lovingly caresses the performers, the
audience, and the sublime, beguiling flower children as they stroll
the grounds and bask in the glow of a weekend of "Music, Love
and Flowers." Hendrix had already stunned audiences in England,
where every rock guitarist, including Pete, instantly understood
that his playing was unmatched. Backstage at Monterey, Pete
confronted Hendrix for stealing his guitar-smashing act, and they

flipped a coin to see who would go on first, neither wanting to follow the other. The Who won and went on, with rocker Eric Burdon announcing, "This is a group that will destroy you completely in more ways than one."[12]

After the opening chords of "Substitute," Keith launched into chaotic smashing—sticks splintering and drums tumbling over—totally in sync with John's driving bass and Pete's propulsive hooks. The band broke through the blues jam haze of the day. They ended their set with their signature aggressive auto-destruction, smashing their instruments and setting off smoke bombs in the mellow California evening.

Writing for *Esquire*, Robert Christgau liked the Who but thought that halfway through the set

> the audience wasn't with them. Then they did "My Generation." The song is not what you'd think of as flower music; it is raucous, hard-driving, hostile. . . . "My Generation" really caught the crowd, and somewhere among the refrains the destruction started. . . . As bassist John Entwistle kept the beat, Daltry [sic] crashed his mike against the cymbals and Townshend thrashed the amplifiers. A smoke bomb exploded. The audience was in pandemonium and the stage crew, which had been magnificent all weekend, was worse. One hero tried to save a mike and nearly lost his head to Townshend's guitar. [Festival producer] Lou Adler, frantic and furious, protected one set of amplifiers. The love crowd was on its feet, screaming and cheering.[13]

Supposedly, backstage Hendrix was heard to mutter, "What can I do for an encore to that?"[14]

Nobody even remembers that the Grateful Dead played next, a set they themselves found forgettable, but rock critic Michael

Lydon declared, "They played pure music, some of the best music of the concert. I have never heard anything in music which could be said to be qualitatively better than the performance of the Dead Sunday night."[15] I suspect he is in the minority. Even members of the Dead demurred. Jerry Garcia lamented, "We came onstage just after The Who finished smashing their equipment onstage for the first time in America. This is aahhh, the audience is devastated. The Who were beautifully theatrical, there's clouds of smoke and explosions and they're clearing away the debris. And so we came out and played our little act—ding ching ding ding—and then Jimi Hendrix comes on after us. We were erased from existence."[16] "[W]e didn't deliver what we could," recalled bassist Phil Lesh. "Though, really, it didn't matter. Between the Who tearing it up, doing a great set, and then destroying the stage at the end of their set, and then Jimi playing a fantastic set and then lighting his guitar on fire . . . what are you gonna remember, who came between them?"[17]

Hendrix's now-legendary performance, capped off by him setting his guitar on fire in an orgiastic ritual, was greeted with mixed reviews. Christgau scathingly condemned him as a "just an Uncle Tom."[18] Most, however, marveled at the performance. Jimi had stolen the Who's act, but gone one better, deeper.

The festival performance did not vault the Who up the charts, but it did introduce them to Californians, especially the other musicians. The band demonstrated that they were now a force to be taken seriously. The guitar smashing had started as an explosive acting-out of emotional catharsis within the confines of the club, the rock 'n' roll show as a place to perform strange behaviors, to let off steam and then return to normal life. As rock becomes something more in 1967, auto-destruction morphs into a statement about society.

Chapter 5

1967

Finding Baba

I can imagine few things more terrifying than being trapped on an airplane on a bad acid trip from California to London.

Pete had been smoking pot regularly since art school. He had been exploring spirituality and alternate explanations of the universe, reading widely about aliens, interplanetary visits, and UFOs. Some of this exploration fit with the general vibe of the counterculture, and some was unique to Pete's own development. Pete had been taking LSD regularly for more than a year at least, a year that was mostly unproductive. He'd had access to Switzerland's Sandoz laboratories acid, but was exposed to San Franciscan Owsley's strains in California. On the way home after playing Monterey, he had the ultimate bad trip on Owsley's new concoction STP with a much more concentrated dose and longer trip than the normal LSD. He told the story repeatedly over the years:

What shook me about acid was when I took what I thought was acid, but turned out to be STP—something that I would never ever take. It was after the Monterey Pop Festival, and I spent more time outside of my body looking inside myself than I've ever spent . . . it was like a hundred years. It was actually a four hour hump, whereas a normal acid hump is about 25–30 minutes . . . you have a hump and then plane off into a nice trip. Well on this STP trip, the hump was about 4 to 5 hours—and it was on an aeroplane over the Atlantic.[1]

I felt that if l had cut off my own head the horrible feeling would go on for eternity because I wasn't in my own body.[2]

It was the most extraordinary drug experience that I have ever been through. It was just absolutely bizarre, like Alice in Wonderland, like extreme mental illness, nothing good about it at all, but so disturbing that I left my body. And I floated up on the ceiling of the aircraft looking down at myself and I'm sitting there and I'm unconscious. It's extremely disturbing and I'm very, very frightened I'm going to die. And when I get home I kinda think about this and I think, I left my body. I just left my body. So I know that I am not my fucking body.[3]

It is striking how, when he retells the story, the details are remarkably consistent, as is his attempt to explain how the border between inside and outside was erased.

Soon after his acid trip, Townshend was introduced to the teachings of Meher Baba by his friend, the artist Mike McInnerney. Clearly ready for—seeking—such a framework for understanding and engaging with the world, Pete found a philosophy and community for his life. Baba had been teaching since the 1920s, even visiting Hollywood in the 1930s, meeting a bevy of stars, but Pete was attracted by the focus on love, surrender, universal harmony—themes that would infuse his work going forward. It's probably not too much to say that Meher Baba is the single greatest influence on Pete from here on out. He tears up his spaceship magazines and devotes himself to following Baba; as he told *Rolling Stone* in 1970: "Meher Baba is the Avatar, God Incarnate on our planet. The Awakener."[4]

Baba's *Discourses* present his teachings and a plan of action for the spiritual seeker, ranging from the esoteric to the practical. McInnerney has written, "For me, the chapter on love provided the most holistic sense of being in the world, making real the idea that everything is connected and that I could recognize this and understand it."[5] From hearing Pete talk and write about Baba, it is not always clear what exactly Baba stands for or believes in. But what is clear is Pete's sense of devotion. From the beginning he screams, "I've found it! . . . This is absolutely IT! Baba is the one." He explains in interviews and in an 8000-word article for *Rolling Stone* how he is "In Love with Meher Baba."[6]

Following Baba, Pete gives up acid, and then, upon discovering that Baba rejects all drugs, reluctantly renounces pot, pronouncing himself drug free for the first time (though not the last). Pot had always been central to Pete's experience of music, going back to his art school days lying around listening to records by Charlie Parker, so this was no small thing. Drugs were, of course, also central to the counterculture, so Pete's public display was also taking a controversial stand. But the whole experience formed the basis for the creation of *Tommy*, which slowly began to emerge in this period.

Perhaps the key issue Pete was exploring that Baba provided answers for was the question of illusion and reality:

What we call "straight" is an illusory "reality." In fact getting high is getting low; going further into the illu-

sion. Reality is beyond our imaginations, we insisting
that we prefer experience to the blissful peace of Universality; wearing blue suede shoes rather than feeling
the Infinite Power of Eternity, of Oneness.[7]

If that was the intellectual problem Pete was wrestling with, it
is clear that Baba provided him with more than an intellectual
solution. Baba delivered a feeling Pete could not get elsewhere,
a feeling he craved at his deepest core: "Only one person on this
earth is capable of an absolutely perfect love for all and everything,
and that is, when earth is fortunate enough to be his illusory
host, the Messiah. The Avatar. He just came and went. Meher
Baba." How does anyone know who they really are? "The key is
that knowledge of his awesome power, awesome knowledge and
bliss he enjoys; that flash, is the basis for the search for my true
self. It sounds light, even camp, but it's not. *It's extremely heavy.*"[8]

Baba also answered Pete's desperate desire for transcendence,
something that recurs throughout his work for the rest of his life,
and for the expression of that transcendence through music, the
music he hears in his head:

From the peace of the original note, the single unmul-
tiplied breath of life, the eternal silent singing that
pervaded all, came this. Us. What are we supposed
to be doing? Here am I, in suburban Twickenham,
skinny, vain, and obsessed by the word "forward"; how
am I equipped to begin to understand Infinite Love?[9]

And Baba's teachings emphasized surrender, the peace that comes
with yielding everything, no longer seeking to answer those
eternal questions, no longer struggling with daily life and infinite
existence. Surrender. "Baba says over and over again that the
shortest route to God realization is by surrendering one's heart
and love to The Master."[10]

These themes—illusion/reality, transcendence, surrender, "Don't worry, be happy"—formed the basis of Pete's obsessions while he was writing *Tommy*. Pete wants to answer the deepest questions, but he also really just wants to feel better. He wants to sound profound, but he also so desperately wants to feel a moment of peace, deep eternal peace. He wants to embrace the profound, ineffable complexities of the entire universe, and he wants it all contained in a simple formula, in one idea, one word, one note.

That whole period feels a bit confused as to the details—as I am sure it was for him—but he was immersed in struggling to break through, psychologically, artistically, and professionally.

Chapter 6

Making *Tommy*

Pete's devotion to his beloved Meher Baba—who took a vow of silence, declaring, "You have had enough of my words, now it is time to live by them"[1]—only went so far. Pete certainly wasn't going to follow him into a lifetime of silence. Pete loved to talk, and to hear himself talk. And in the late 1960s, he had a new forum for talking. If the rock world of the early 1960s depended on the pop star–making machinery to promote the latest acts, that industrial system had evolved so that rock journalists were part of the process, now visible, allies, artists/politicos in their own right, pushed by the new journalism and their countercultural immersion. The rock business still depended on an army of "squares"—press agents, accountants, managers—but those people now dressed like scenesters and partook of the atmosphere and ethos. In England especially, there was a vast apparatus for the selling of rock music, with fan magazines churning out promotional material based on constructed images of photos and stories to connect pop stars with their fans. Radio and TV fueled a crazed industry of pop stardom, with an insatiable audience ready for whatever the industry could produce.

However, the rock promotion world was undergoing a transformation, along with the rest of the rock world. Starting in the mid-1960s, a parallel media of serious rock journalism began to emerge, with *Crawdaddy, Mojo Navigator, Rolling Stone*, and *Creem* offering more adult and analytical coverage, with critics writing about lyrical significance and social issues connected to rock. Much of the established and emerging British musical press (*NME, Melody Maker, Hit Parader*, etc.) began to make the transition, straddling both sides. There had never been "rock journalists" and "rock critics" before: "professional writers who interviewed musicians, followed bands and individual performers as they toured, and sometimes lived the lifestyle of the rockers whom they wrote about. Critics reviewing albums became arbiters of taste."[2] Alongside the new provocative music of the period, these magazines marked the shift from rock 'n' roll as a subset of pop to rock as a genre and world of its own.[3]

Pete was comfortable in both the old-style pop and new rock journalist's world. He was infatuated with the whole pop process, and he saw himself as a creator at all stages, not just songwriting and performing. The Who embraced the pop world, but also sent it up. As an artist inspired by the Pop Art movement, Pete both partook of and commented on it, most obviously with *The Who Sell Out*, which placed the crass commercial aspect of rock right up front for both gentle mockery and instant nostalgia. The Pop Art process included the marketplace. In fact, Pete continued to defend pop while the musical world moved on to rock. The new generation of magazines helped craft the distinction between rock and pop, a line that Pete continually straddled, aware that his pop success depended on his rock credentials. And his artistic ambitions continued to embrace pop interventions and commentary. This is really key to understanding his motivation and vision of his place in the world. He saw himself as an artist, but immersed in the commercial world, both by temperament (he was "apolitical"), but also by ambition (he wanted success and money). His art was deeply engaged, but eschewed closed endings, meanings. Pete lacked the discipline to keep to a scripted character. No doubt he played the marketing game, fulfilling his role as teen pop star when necessary. However, Pete also acknowledged Bob Dylan's importance in creating the social role of the rock star. As Dave Marsh writes, "Dylan suggested a context in which rock singers not only could establish their seriousness, but one in which the standard adolescent assertion that something is terribly wrong in the adult world could be developed as an implicit critique of society. That context was pop itself . . ."[4] Pete came to see the rock press as an important conduit to his audience and an important player in its own right in the rock community.

If some might claim that "Townshend's magazine interviews made him appear artsy, self-conscious, and pretentious,"[5] writers, as you can imagine, absolutely loved it, seeing Pete "as unpredictable as a badly made Roman candle"[6] who "begins firing sentences at you from his machine-gun mind."[7] Keith Altham at *NME*, one of Pete's interlocutors, told readers, "There is no doubt that Pete is incredibly easy to interview although his deeper philosophical ideas often weigh down his argument and you find yourself lost in a sea of imponderables."[8] A sea of imponderables, indeed. And when the interview format does not prove expansive enough, Pete even takes on regular writing gigs to propound on these imponderables. Throughout the era, Pete regularly sat for long interviews or wrote his own columns for *Rolling Stone* and *Melody Maker*. He appreciated what rock journalists did perhaps more than any other rock star of the era because he thought like a rock critic: that is, he thought as much about how to connect with an audience as he did about the song itself.

Pete called himself "the greatest rock critic in the world. I was two people—someone who sat down and wrote a song for a particular purpose, and then somebody who looked at it and saw something totally different."[9] He told the interviewer for *Crawdaddy* who dared question his insights, "I'm the only person who knows what rock & roll's all about. I'm the only true rock critic."[10]

Pete understood the songwriting process as twofold: the inspiration and the understanding. As he told an interviewer in 1974, "that's why Bob Dylan doesn't know what to say when people ask him about one of his songs—because he doesn't fucking know what it's all about. I know, because I'm on the outside reacting to it, and whatever it means to me is it. But he doesn't. How could he? All he did was write it."[11] Brilliant. "How could he? All he did was write it."

Pete would use his interviews with rock critics like Greil Marcus, Dave Marsh, and Cameron Crowe to sound out ideas both about his current work and about the world around them. His insights into his own work are as perceptive as anyone's; his insights into the world, not so much. Years later, Pete explained:

> Time spent with a journalist was always valuable to me. The fact that sometimes journalists might have misread my openness, my eagerness to fly my wildest and flimsiest ideas past them before they'd even properly formed in my mind, did not bother me. I was reading their faces while I brainstormed, looking for a reaction. I was building my ideas in the time I had available, knowing that—in any case, as a natural part of my career—I had to do the interviews to keep fans engaged and to keep the record company aware that we were indeed working on making new records and had new ideas. I figured I might as well allow my interviews to do double duty. I began to rely on, and made deep lasting friendships with, a number of journalists that (our respective professional career roles of rock star and rock critic aside) were based on reciprocal respect and a truly symbiotic interdependence.[12]

Pete had a complex relationship with the emerging counterculture, but he felt as one with the rock press wing. The critics were exploring rock in ways that he was. He didn't see them simply as cogs in the promotional machine—though he accepted, even respected, that whole process. He didn't see them as on the other side of a creative divide, with him as the genius and them as the parasites. He saw them as men—and they seem to have all been men—who were on the same journey of intellectual engagement with cultural matters . . . matters that reached from the song into every corner of human endeavor and beyond.

I can't think of another artist who revealed his process so casually, even carelessly, to the public as he was thinking and working through things. It's fun to watch him stumble through his process and into something.

The interviews, many of them seemingly quick and haphazard, are often just a bit too revealing, or so it seems, but that is the currency of the pop music scene infrastructure, like the Hollywood fan magazines of the 1920s and 1930s, taking you inside, revealing the (seemingly) true inner workings of the business and the star's innermost thoughts to you and you alone (with your fellow enlightened insider friends). The industry demands it; pop stardom depends on it. The Beatles crafted their personas to publicly perform their carefree commentary on the world, embracing the whole phenomenon in their films as performances of that star-making machinery, which become the very topic of their movies. They expose themselves completely while revealing as little as possible. Dylan renders himself opaque; his lyrics so deeply comment on the world, but he refuses to comment further outside his songs, desperately fending off any interpretation that threatens to stick. Jerry Garcia, Joan Baez, and others embrace their roles as spokespeople for an emerging, developing intellectual and political generation.

Pete sees himself within this whole context, as artist, as product, as pop manufacturer and pop commodity, as representative of a generation, but also as a captive to a fickle, dangerous, stupid, cruel, demanding audience. He once claimed to hate his audience because they are his employer, and of course he hates his boss—a sentiment that reaches toward a deeper commentary on the nature of stardom, revealing a truth about his own feelings, but doesn't actually blame or pathologize the fans, nor (cannily enough) does it threaten his future sales.[13] And it positions him as a working-class bloke, just like his fans! Finally, while presented tongue slightly in cheek, it does have the ring of truth, at least a little bit, about it.

Pete loves to reveal whatever is on his mind at the time of an interview. I'm sure there was some degree of calculation about the role of the press and his own relationship with it; Pete was quite self-aware about the whole business. But he really delights in sharing what he is thinking about at that very moment. He loves to talk about himself, as long as it concerns what he is thinking about and working on right then.

And so we get to see the story of *Tommy* emerging, and we can see what initially concerns Pete and how his concept evolved from his earlier interviews back in 1967 discussing his first experiments with creating longer compositions. It's really quite amazing to watch Pete create *Tommy*. There is an extraordinary historical record, something that I doubt exists for any artist of the period, and for few of any period. Pete gave interviews throughout the process of writing *Tommy* that guide us through the whole process as the opera is emerging from his mind. The first song he writes is "Amazing Journey," and the story develops from there. Pete first settles on "deaf, dumb, and blind boy," which he reveals as the working title. In fact, Pete announces numerous titles, most often *Amazing Journey* and *Deaf, Dumb and Blind Boy*, landing on *Tommy*, which Pete loved because of its multiple references: "I got Tommy's name from mid-air, but it suited. The middle letters were OM which was aptly mystical, and it was an English name associated with the war and heroism. It was also fairly close to To-Me, again you can see the obvious spiritual bent."[14]

The key public moment comes in the wee hours after an August 1968 gig at the Fillmore in San Francisco. There is no record of how the gig went, but let's go with Pete at 2:00 a.m. to *Rolling Stone* to hang out with the Jefferson Airplane's Jack Casady and friends, snort some blow, and start talking with publisher Jann Wenner of *Rolling Stone* while Wenner turns on the tape recorder, and Pete starts talking. A more circumspect rock star might have spent the night *without* the tape recorder running. To Pete, Wenner is an ally, a participant in the whole scene, the whole project of the counterculture, so why not spend the night snorting lines of cocaine and talking about the project that is occupying your mind? Coked out of his mind—you can hear it, see it all while reading through the interview—the immediacy jumps out at you.[15]

By early 1968, the Who were busy building the opera in their studio in England, but also playing local gigs and touring the United States. Kit Lambert had encouraged Pete to explore something more ambitious, and it was all jelling. The project that has been germinating is now taking root but is not yet finished. And they had only left the studio to tour the States because they had to pay the bills. Then Pete meets the right drug and the right interlocuter with all the time in the world.

Pete tells Jann, "Well, the album concept in general is complex. I don't know if I can explain it in my condition, at the moment." But he does proceed to explain. The concept is "a pretty far-out thing, actually." Pete wants to translate music into feelings into music, and the deaf, dumb, and blind boy is the vehicle: "He's seeing things basically as vibrations which we translate as music. That's really what we want to do: create this feeling that when you listen to the music you can actually become aware of the boy, and aware of what he is all about, because we are creating him as we play." This really is the crux: how to get the purest essence of music, the purest experience: "But it's very, very endearing to me because the thing is . . . inside; the boy sees things musically and in dreams, and nothing has got any weight at all. He is touched from the outside, and he feels his mother's touch, he feels his father's touch, but he just interprets them as music."

The whole project originates in the pursuit of the purest form of music as deliverance, transcendence. In part this is because Pete is a person who hears and feels music differently than the rest of us, spending his whole life trying to capture and share what is inside his head, inside his body. He wouldn't be the first. His contemporary Brian Wilson also was someone who simply feels life differently because of the sounds in his head. I suppose musical geniuses throughout the ages share this quality. But there is something else going on with the evolution of this particular project. In the earliest drafts, the boy is born deaf, dumb, and blind so that Pete can avoid the traumatic event that shuts the boy in on himself. But why? Why does Pete so desperately desire this? In a sense, this is the thread that runs through his life.

As Pete relates the story that is still developing in his mind to Jann, he goes from the scene of the boy feeling his mother's and father's touch to the boy being forsaken, rejected, abused. The father resents the kid's abnormality, demanding Tommy hear him. However, Pete loves what the boy is doing: "The kid, of course, can't hear him. He's groovin' in this musical thing, this incredible musical thing; he'll be out of his mind." Then his father becomes more insistent—"really uptight now"—and Pete tells Jann that John will write the song that introduces the abuse of Tommy. Pete won't write the song of pain, of reality intruding on Tommy's groovin':

> The kid won't respond, he just smiles. The father
> starts to hit him, and at this moment the whole thing

becomes incredibly realistic. On one side you have the dreamy music of the boy wasting through his nothing life. And on the other you have the reality of the father outside, uptight, but now you've got blows, you've got communication. The father is hitting the kid; musically then I want the thing to break out, hand it over to Keith—"This is your scene man, take it from here."

Now Keith is enlisted to handle the real world, to lash out, to pound on his drums in a representation of the beating of Tommy.[16] And Tommy (or Pete) simply retreats into the comfort of music: "And the kid doesn't catch the violence. He just knows that some sensation is happening. He doesn't feel the pain, he doesn't associate it with anything. He just accepts it."

Then comes the uncle: "The uncle is a bit of a perv, you know . . . and the uncle comes in and starts to go through a scene with the kid's body, you know, and the boy experiences sexual vibrations, you know, sexual experience, and again it's just basic music; it's interpreted as music, and it is nothing more than music." Why? What is this about? "It's got no association with sleaziness or with undercover or with any of the things normally associated with sex. None of the romance, none of the visual stimulus, none of the sound stimulus. Just basic touch. It's meaningless. Or not meaningless; you just don't react, you know." Well, actually, I don't know.

What is going on here? From a plot perspective, we can see the movement, the challenges, and obstacles for our protagonist. After the album came out, Pete insisted over and over in interviews that the story is not "sick." And I take him at this word. This is not mere shock or titillation. But he needs John and Keith to tap into these abusive characters. He cannot write them himself. All he can connect with at this stage of the process is that the abuse is "meaningless." By initially conceiving of the boy as born this way, then outsourcing the abuse to Entwistle, Pete avoids the trauma. There is no primal scene, no parents silencing the child. It all just happens.

Pete goes on to try to explain how the boy escapes from his inner cage. At this point, Pete sees it as a gradual realization. He hasn't developed the "smash the mirror" moment yet. But he has a strong idea of the next part of the story, of Tommy's life:

> This is the difficult jump. It's going to be extremely difficult, but we want to try to do it musically. . . . The music has got to explain what happens, that the boy elevates and finds something which is incredible. To us, it's nothing to be able to see and hear and speak, but to him, it's absolutely incredible and overwhelming; this is what we want to do musically. Lyrically, it's quite easy to do it; in fact, I've written it out several times. It makes great poetry, but so much depends on the music, so much. I'm hoping that we can do it. The lyrics are going to be okay, but every pitfall of what we're trying to say lies in the music, lies in the way we play the music, the way we interpret, the way things are going during the opera.

I just absolutely love this; I love being on the inside while Pete is creating. I love that he is vulnerable enough to explain the process, coked-up enough to admit the challenges, filled with ego and ambition, but himself loving the challenge of creating something that captures his vision, his sense, the music he hears in his head. The result here is the song "Sensation," and, like so many of the songs, it fucking works. He pulls it off. The Who pull it off.

Later in the night, Pete talks about his family: "The whole incredible thing about my parents is that I just can't place their effect on me, and yet I know that it's there. I can't say how they affected me. When people find out that my parents are musicians, they ask how it affected me. Fucked if I know; musically, I can't place it, and I can't place it in any other way." Pete's father was a saxophonist in The Squadronaires, the dance orchestra for the Royal Air Force, and his mother had been a singer. Much later in life, in his autobiography, Pete could answer some of these questions, especially regarding the deep and formative place of his parents' musical life on his own. He was able to assess the impact of his parents' volatile marriage and two-year separation, during which he was sent to live with his abusive grandmother. He could face how "incredibly exposed, alone and unprotected" he felt during those years.[17]

But here he sees no connection of his childhood abuse to the story he has just told to Jann Wenner. Pete is twenty-three years old, working out his trauma by transmuting it into art, in the classically Freudian definition of sublimation. But he is clearly nowhere near aware that he is telling his own story. It's worth noting also that while Pete mentions the spiritual aspect of the album, nowhere in the roughly 15,196 words Pete spoke that night does he mention Meher Baba.

"Pinball Wizard" was released as a single in March 1969, before the album was finished. The album came out in May, and the Who toured the United Kingdom and United States to support it. The album and singles charted well, and reviews were mostly positive. Outside the rock world, the album was noticed because some found it "distasteful" or "sick" because of the abuse of the autistic character. But the rock world took the whole effort seriously, appreciating the expansive nature of the effort, if not all the results.

Not all were impressed with the end product. Pete invited his friend rock critic Nik Cohn to listen to the early mixes, and Cohn found the whole project a bit sodden and portentous, suggesting Pete find a way to lighten and liven things up. From their encounter, Pete wrote "Pinball Wizard"—one of the last pieces of the story. In his review for the *New York Times*, Cohn still found the storyline "unimpressive" and disparaged "all those religious-political-mystic overtones" as "straight off some intellectual conveyor belt, 100 stock rock parables for our time," But he also declared, " 'Tommy' is just possibly the most important work that anyone has yet done in rock" and embraced the musical gusto of the album:

> It hardly ever flags. In turns, it is fierce and funny, schmaltzy and sour. Always imaginative. Well, it also has its moments of pomposity. . . . Yet the individual songs aren't really the point; it's the sum effect that's the clincher. So much stamina, such range and musical invention—this might just be the first pop masterpiece.[18]

The critic Albert Goldman, as a scholar of Wagner and Thomas de Quincy and the designer of Columbia University's first course on popular culture, brought a highbrow imprimatur to his rock reviews for an audience beyond rock fans. Writing for *Life* magazine, he hailed *Tommy* as "a full-length pop opera that for sheer power, invention and brilliance of performance outstrips anything that has ever come out of a rock recording studio." Goldman situates *Tommy* within a larger musical tradition than rock, referencing John Cage and Karlheinz Stockhausen as well as *Sgt. Pepper*, and noting for *Life*'s readers that "though labeled 'opera,' *Tommy* is closer to an 18th Century oratorio or passion (a fact signaled by the grave baroque bass and harpsichord-like shakes of the overture)." He claims that Townshend has achieved what great artists of the twentieth century have been seeking: "to cultivate from the popular arts a new serious art that combines the beauty with the strength of native roots." Like most reviewers, he has trouble summarizing the plot and some of the themes ("Considered as myth, *Tommy* is intriguing and absurd . . ."). But he raves about the formal perfection of the composition and performance:

> Considered as music, *Tommy* is magnificent, the final crystallization of the hard-rock style in an art as dry, hard, lucid, as unashamedly conventional and finely impersonal as the music of the most severe classicist. Thanks to this mastered style—antithetical to the eclectic jumble of most "serious" rock—The Who runs on a clear track through all the kinky complications of its text. From the first jubilant notes of John Entwistle's horn to the final 20th Century-Fox apotheosis, the music roars with searing energy—that Who energy suggestive of jet flight, rocket flight, all the swift, cool, cruel velocities of the Age of Speed.

Goldman marvels at "The Who's power source . . . rock's only super-drummer, Keith Moon" who "is always upping the excitement with chattering Sten-gun bursts, heavy VC rocket booms and abrupt splashes of fuming acid." From that "power source," the "whole album seems dedicated to the proposition: *Energy is beauty*."[19]

Goldman made even grander claims in a review for the *New York Times*, referencing Beethoven, Bach, Wagner, and Verdi: "What 'Tommy' proclaims with the first blast of its Beethovenish horn is the red dawn of revolt. The love days are over, it trumpets, now come the days of wrath. War is the opera's real theme, war of generation against generation, war between the younger generation and its own leaders." Goldman predicted that the opera "prefigures . . . the final confrontation when blood will flow in the streets and the seats of power will be dynamited."[20]

Well, maybe.

Chapter 7

The Album

Childhood, Cure, Fame

The production notes for the recording sessions in 1968–69 divide the album's tracks into three sections: Childhood, Cure, Fame.

Childhood

Pete sets Tommy up. The "Overture" prepares us beautifully for what we are in for. Staccato emphases, rising crescendos, dropping down into aahs and peaceful acoustic strumming by Pete. Keith is restrained, but building as the organ comes in. John's French Horn signals that this is majestic . . . then the strumming gets frantic—electric through the left channel and acoustic through the right—then steady as Pete sings, "Captain Walker didn't come home, his unborn child would never know him." The mournful horn and Pete's voice announces, "It's a boy, Mrs. Walker/It's a boy."

After the war, Captain Walker returns, finds his wife in another man's arms, murders that man. Mother and father demand of Tommy: "You didn't hear it, you didn't see it, you never heard

49

it, not a word of it, you won't say nothing to no one, never tell a soul what you know is the truth."

How could a boy fulfill this edict? How does a boy, a boy who wants to please, carry out that order? Every sound he makes, word he speaks, gesture he takes, threatens to reveal the truth he carries inside. So he must shut down all means of communication, all possibilities that he might violate the pact. There is no way to guarantee that he won't slip up. Imagine the pressure.

Imagine witnessing this crime—in the mirror, as Pete reminds us, though the song does not make that obvious—and then being told you didn't see what you saw, that what you know to be true is not true, that you can never speak of this. The "never speak" order is enough, really. That's all it takes to make communication fraught going forward. You dare not speak of anything at all lest something slip out. But the deeper edict, that you never experienced what you just experienced, makes all human interaction impossible.

The truth you know is not the truth.

Did Tommy calculate, weigh the odds, sit and figure out how best to go on living while fulfilling his orders? Whether done so thoughtfully, with full measure of all the factors and variables, or in an instant, in less than an instant, with no thought at all, but only by instinct, feeling, amygdala, and central nervous system, like a nematode responding to stimuli, Tommy takes the only path he can.

It's interesting that this is all Pete's storytelling to start, as he sings all the opening songs. His voice, a bit thin and reedy compared with Roger's, the story plaintive and mournful, but still inviting. It's as if Pete didn't trust Roger to sing the songs, they were so important, so personal. And it was really with this album that Pete began to respect Roger, crediting him for bringing something to the album, the character, and stage performance that went beyond what Pete had conceived.

Finally, Roger comes in to sing for us the story of the boy. Pete lets go a bit and sends Tommy on his amazing journey—"Each sensation makes a note / In my symphony." This was the original song, the germ of the story. This is the story that Pete really wants to tell, the story of a limitless interior life, unconcerned with the outside, where the real world outside is illusion and the world of sensation is the only reality—and that reality is beautiful, where sensation become music. "Sensation" is an interesting word choice here, a word that will return later, with its own song at the end of side three, when Tommy is liberated and launched into the world. Here, though, it means both the physical act of stimulation and the interior feeling of that stimulus. And in Pete's hands that external force is instantly and painlessly and beautifully transformed, transmuted into music, one perfect, eternal note in a symphony of such notes. Each act of violation of Tommy becomes yet another note.

Pete creates an external projection of himself and proceeds to let the world have its way with him. He wanted a character who was cut off from the world—disabled—in order to get at the purest, most direct experience of music as a spiritual experience: "Sickness will surely take the mind, where minds can't usually go, come on the amazing journey, and learn all you should know." He wants his character's mind to be free, ready to receive music in "pure and easy" forms. Tommy stares into the mirror, going deeper and deeper into self.

That is why originally the character was deaf, dumb, and blind at birth. Pete was not interested in writing about trauma; he wanted to avoid it altogether. Most interesting to me is that, in Pete's first interviews discussing the project as he is writing the work, Tommy starts out having been born that way. Pete creates him in that form so that he can do whatever he wants with him. Pete does not want Tommy to have any past, any messy story that will distract from what is about to happen. You can see Pete thinking this through . . . . What if I take a boy who is uncorrupted by the world and impose the world upon him, how will he respond to the music I create? Initially, Pete does not want to get into how Tommy got that way. It's all about transformation and release, without having to look back. Can't I just be reborn? Can't I just create myself, here and now, without having to confront the pain that I am in because of what I have experienced? And I think a bit of that wish stays with Pete throughout the various incarnations of *Tommy*, even today.

Pete sends him out to be molested, abused, subject to the whims of cruel and unthinking adults. He sends Tommy out into the world with no protection. From here on out, Tommy does not exist. There is no Tommy anymore. Abusers and misguided parents, charlatans, and fellow desperate humans can all do as they please, because Tommy does not carry with him a human soul. And Pete can breathe easy, for just a moment.

Pete needs Tommy to suffer so that he does not have to. Tommy shuts down so Pete can keep going. How does Pete not shut down? In fact, he cannot handle Uncle Ernie and Cousin Kevin, characters whose actions he found so painful that he could not write their songs, sloughing them off on Entwistle, whose brilliant, twisted mind could come up with the exact mix of comedy and horror to make the songs work as songs rather than death sentences. Pete's one-note cannot contain those two characters.

Imagine the cost it carried for Pete to do this to Tommy. To create a character to suffer, so that Pete could get a slight relief from his own suffering. To see Pete stumbling through the process, stumbling toward a full character and story, is to see him wrestling with his own self. It's beautiful to watch, really, to see a young man willing to share so much in public—maybe full of hubris and rock star puffery, not to mention cocaine, but willing nonetheless—exposing the process as he wrenches himself open, places his trauma out for all to see (without, of course, quite knowing that is what he is doing exactly).

As I struggle with Pete's interpretations and explanations, it occurs to me that the role of the critic, the analyst, the historian is to say, I know something that you, the artist, do not. I can see through you, into you, where you cannot see. You need me to explain to you what you are really trying to do. As Pete said of Dylan, "he doesn't fucking know what it's all about. . . . How could he? All he did was write it."[1]

Pete is endearing, because he does that so explicitly himself. He is constantly analyzing himself, often with deep insight. But the historian in me—and the child inside me who listened to *Tommy* a few thousand times—we know something he doesn't. We can see what he cannot, how his blind spot is the source of the whole of *Tommy*. *Tommy* emerges from the place Pete cannot go, where he cannot see, in himself.

Cure

"Sparks" is a beautiful, psychedelic trip into the interior, but we don't really know what's going on. We really are taking our own journey with this instrumental—a journey that approximates Tommy's, I suppose, as all we can do is fill in our own fantasy. We never get to know what is going on inside Tommy. The mirror and the pinball machine are the only hints of an interior life.

When Tommy is told, "you didn't hear it" etc., he wisely shuts down. But what is going on inside? Does he know that his reality is the truth, but because there will be no outside confirmation, he must shut down? Is there an internal struggle, or does he resolve it peacefully by simply refusing to engage? The story is told from those outside. We never get his internal story. Even later, once he is talking, he never tells what was going on inside all those years.

We see Tommy experiencing life, disconnected as he is, most powerfully in "Christmas," which might be the best song on the album: Daltrey's voice soaring, almost falsetto, earnest and strong, without forcing anything, complemented by aahs and oohs from the band; Pete's delicious little accenting lick on guitar, followed by the clang of his strum; Keith covering the kit, with every fill, propelling each section. In the middle of the song comes the breakdown—with Pete's rasping voice introducing the insistent, pleading "Tommy can you hear me?" and Roger introducing the boy's inner voice: "See me, feel me, touch me, heal me," equally insistent, equally pleading, but achingly heartbreaking. Then the return to the verse, more insistent, propulsive, Roger's yowl punctuating the dense accompaniment. In a sense, the song doesn't stand on its own, because it ties together the threads of the story so far, but it creates a fully developed vignette of the character in his world. It contains all the elements of the best Who songs—the power, gracefulness, dynamics—and is as beautiful as anything Pete has written. And while the family celebrates around him, Tommy sits alone, unaware, locked in his "eternal grave."

Mostly we see Tommy acted upon, most vividly in the Entwistle-written songs "Cousin Kevin" and "Fiddle About," where Tommy is brutalized and sodomized by his relatives. Entwistle's songs always seem like novelties, throwaways, but they burrow under the skin to settle and unsettle. Tommy is at the mercy of others in the other songs, too, as his parents take him to various charlatans and quacks who promise to heal him. Perhaps this is the worst part of it all. To assuage their own guilt, his parents and relatives must continually torture him, because to admit what they did is to have their whole lives come crashing down. They know they are the cause of his ailment but cannot tell anyone who is supposed to cure him. And this is never brought up at any time in the whole album. We never get a real sense of the parents as characters, perhaps only the growing desperation as his mother sings, "Can you feel my temper rise, rise, rise . . ." Finally the mother smashes the mirror. And that's it; Tommy is cured.

In his pursuit of enlightenment, purity, nirvana, Pete wants to eliminate all distractions, pain, suffering. He talks often about how spirituality does not provide an "escape clause"; you don't get a shortcut bypassing the normal human experiences. Meher Baba—whom he credits as "Avatar" on the album cover—brings him only a way to face the reality of himself directly. But, ultimately, Pete desperately wants to smash the mirror, be done with it all, and move on. Smashing the mirror sure seems like an escape clause, a shortcut.

For Tommy, when he breaks through, what is the nature of that event? Has he transcended? Has he simply given up holding tight to his own version of events? Does he give up what he knows is the truth? We move right into "Sensation"—a word no longer meaning the feelings of being acted upon, but representing Tommy's newfound power in the world. Tommy launches right into being the Avatar, the Messiah, fully "god-realised."

Does anyone even ask him his story once he is released? No one seems to have compassion for Tommy. They are all impressed, in awe even, but do they bother to ask what was going on all those years? After all, Tommy does not go to the cops to report a murder. He allows his family to continue in his life, even to the extent of them exploiting him and his fame. His parents were frustrated, scared, they knew how he got the way he was, they knew what they did to cause it. What happens to that fear once he is released?

Tommy barely pauses to enjoy his new freedom, this "new vibration," before he instantly claims godhood for himself: "I'm a sensation . . . I know the answer . . . I am the Light." From "I'm free/and freedom tastes of reality" to "I'm free/And I'm waiting for you to follow me," we go from a character who is fully internal, locked in, and inaccessible to us to one who is fully external, acting in the world as he pleases, and still inaccessible to us.

Fame

"I'm Free" tells us that "you'd laugh and say 'nothing's that simple' "—and it is right, nothing is that simple. It tells us to just let go. Nothing and no one can do this for you. To be free, you just have to claim your freedom. Is it will? Surrender? Submission to a higher power? Take actions? If it is all so simple, then why can't/don't/won't we all do it? And why, Pete, are you still a tormented artist? (Or are you? Have you finally found the key?) It goes to the nature of the desire for god, the desire to submit to a master, but without choosing the escape clause or installing an authority. Pete sticks with Baba, who really does seem as good as any, though, to me, no more compelling than any other. But the song captures the whole of Pete's perspective—ultimately, just let go. "Don't worry, be happy," as Meher Baba says and Pete repeats throughout his life. Like many great spiritual insights, it's simultaneously inspired and insipid. But the song builds powerfully, and Roger's voice is at its peak of range and fluidity.

The fame of Tommy—and of the Who—presents an instant challenge to that freedom. In Pete's case, this challenge came from the young people coming of age in 1969, when the rock audience is buying albums, attending Who shows at the Fillmores East and West and gearing up for "An Aquarian Exposition: 3 Days of Peace & Music" at Max Yasgur's farm in Bethel, New York, outside Woodstock. Pete provided one of the more notorious incidents at Woodstock during the Who's set in the predawn hour of Day Two. As the band finished their new single "Pinball Wizard," in the middle of performing the newly released *Tommy*, the Yippie political activist Abbie Hoffman jumped on the stage and grabbed the mic to protest the arrest and ten-year prison sentence of the White Panther Party's leader for marijuana possession:

Abbie: "I think this is a pile of shit! While John Sinclair rots in prison!

Pete: "Fuck off! Fuck off my stage!"

The crowd cheered, but it wasn't clear who they were cheering for, as Pete could barely be heard. A couple of bursts of guitar.

Pete: "I can dig it" (sounding tired, resigned, aloof).

More cheering. The Who launched into "Do You Think It's Alright?" from *Tommy*. Pete tuned up.

Pete: "The next fucking person that walks across this stage is gonna get fucking killed, alright?"

Cheering. Tuning up.

Pete: "You can laugh. I mean it!"

More tuning up.[2]

Some accounts have Townshend literally kicking Hoffman in the ass, while others claim he struck Hoffman with his guitar, whacked him on the head, or poked him like a bayonet. Dave Marsh, in his Who biography, writes, "Townsend put one of his Dr. Martin boots squarely into Hoffman's ass, swatted him with his Gibson SG and, as the Yippie fell into the photographers' pit, played on."[3] Accounts of the incident—and the set—differ, but, Marsh writes, "just as they were finishing, with 'We're Not Gonna Take It,' with Roger's last cries of 'See me, feel me, touch me, heal me' echoing over the hills, the sun burst up over the horizon, dazzling the crowd."[4]

Pete was already cranky, having taken an inadvertent dose of acid, hiked a mile through the mud, and fought with the promoters to get paid—forcing the them to fly in their bank manager to open the bank to get payment. Pete: "then we got there and just started to pick up vibes that were just great. I must admit if you went out of the section where the musicians were, forgot that you were there to work, it was great, but every now and then you'd think, 'I'm part of the sideshow, I'm selling the soft drinks here.'"[5] No film footage, and only scattered, fragmentary photographs, exist of the incident because Pete was already so out of control that he had attacked Michael Wadleigh, head filmmaker, on the stage. The crew were told to hold back until later in the set.[6]

Pete kicked Abbie Hoffman off the stage, and "the sun rose as the Who ended with their set with 'My Generation,' to which Pete added a coda of *Tommy* themes, new riffs, and sound effects as he hammered his guitar on the stage before hurling it, still live, into the pit."[7] Henry Diltz, official photographer, watched the scene unfold from the catwalk in front of the stage but placed three feet below: "Pete Townshend picked up his guitar and went boink [gestures as pushing the guitar rather than chopping] and hit [Hoffman] on the back of the neck and ran offstage and that was that . . ."[8] Almost immediately, and regularly in the years afterward, Townshend claimed he overreacted, that he should have let Hoffman have his say.[9] But the incident gets to the heart of one of the main conflicts within the counterculture. And, ironically, the Who's *Tommy* both predicts and enacts that tension. Perhaps it is not going too far to see the battle being played out as to who will get to lead, what is the nature of this movement.

Pete talks continually throughout his career about the relationship between himself and his audience, how while they are watching and thinking about him, he watches them from the stage. *Tommy* predicts what he sees happening at Woodstock and after, the creation of a passive audience that desperately wants to be led. At the same time, the audience is where he places his hope. Marsh claims that "*Tommy* was speaking directly to a vast international audience which in many ways used the opera to symbolize its sense of power, spirituality and—ultimately—its intention to transform not only itself but the entire world."[10]

But Pete wrestled with this reality. "There is an incredible set of paradoxes surrounding the whole generation," Pete noted. "It's an observation made from the stage, as if we were in a cage. You're being looked at, but you're also in the position for observation."[11] He criticizes the evolution of the rock audience by the end of the 1960s, as it seems the concert—even a concert as grand as Woodstock—becomes simply a way to say "I was there," to affirm one's status and identity as a rock fan, and an album becomes "a signal of allegiance through possession."[12] At the very moment of the Who's greatest artistic triumph and popular success, the relationship between the band and its serious fans was in danger of becoming "a bond of passive consumerism."[13]

What, then, does "We're not gonna take it" mean? The chant is a protest, but it is a protest against Tommy himself, against the rock star as savior, rejecting any possible escape or emergence from bondage. Tommy becomes the villain of the piece? What? That seems like the final insult, one more abuse for him to suffer. Why is the resolution so unsatisfying, and yet not? Yes, the songs redeem everything, so we should start there. "I'm Free" and "We're Not Gonna Take It" are as beautiful and powerful as anything Pete has ever written. With those songs, we emerge free ourselves and reclaim our power against all abusers, all who hold us down. But it has always been so unsatisfying to me, what I still refuse to accept, that there is no reckoning with the people who did this to him. Are we supposed to simply accept this as a metaphor for what all children must finally accept as they grow up—that their parents are just human, who "did the best they could"?

The song clearly wrestles with Pete's current state as avatar of a generation, so lucid, insightful, and eager to lead, while rejecting the responsibility and watching himself stumble in and out of spiritual devotion—the lures of the flesh are just too strong to resist forever. The pain is all just too much. The pain is always there, and Pete wants deliverance. And here he is, thrust into the role (grasping at the role) of the voice. As Marsh quotes Pete, "I've never felt like anybody's hero. . . . But I have felt like a lot of people's voice."[14] He is the guide, the leader, but perhaps a fraud. It all gnaws at him, that perhaps he has taken a shortcut, he is unworthy of his role, and, looking out at the sea of faces, they are unworthy of him.

The 400,000 at Woodstock—who sing along in unison, in public, about how they were not going to take it, they were not going to be led by a hollow charlatan up on the stage—and, yet, here they are, as the sun is coming up, enacting their role. What is their role? Are they to come together in peace, love, and harmony with the Who on stage guiding them for those moments? Or should they reject the Who, rock stars who would not take the stage until their money was helicoptered in (and, wisely, after all, because the promoters were not to be trusted)? Are they the "thousands who want to come and be brainwashed," as Townshend described his fans just a month before Woodstock?[15]

Despite his frustrations with the limits of rock, Pete also embraced the powerful moments that came on first tour playing *Tommy*: "I will never forget that tour, the finale of *Tommy* never failed to mesmerize me along with the audience. It always felt to me like a prayer. I always felt myself full of Meher Baba when we performed it."[16] And "I've seen moments in Who concerts where the vibrations were becoming so pure that I thought the world was just going to stop, the whole thing was just becoming so unified. But could never reach that state because in the back of their minds everybody knew that the group was going to have to stop soon, or they'd got to get home, or catch the last bus or something—it's a ridiculous situation."[17]

I love that: "It's a ridiculous situation."

Ultimately, reality intrudes. Rock cannot challenge the world outside the communal moment of shared experience. The songs deliver freedom, but only at the moment. That is the power—and limits—of the song.

Chapter 8

Tommy Lives

In recording the album, Pete had insisted the production be reproducible onstage—so no string or horn sections. Quickly, both the Who and the audience discovered that *Tommy* worked live—perhaps even better than on the album—because the Who were always a much better band live, where their full force and fury, "their unequaled ferocity and power"[1] were realized.

The Who continued to tour with *Tommy* as the highlight of the show, usually taking up the middle of the set. You can hear a bit in *Live at Leeds* (1970), the album that cemented their new reputation as rock's most powerful live act. Nik Cohn noted that the rock listener was finally getting "the full force of the Who": while *Tommy* was "rock's first formal masterpiece," the live album was "the definitive hard-rock holocaust."[2] Their performance at the Isle of Wight Festival in 1970 became instantly legendary (a recording was released finally in 1996 that confirms how powerful the whole opera was live).

The Who's June 1970 performance at the Metropolitan Opera solidified the movement of the opera out of the rock world and into a larger social phenomenon. Reviews were solid, and mainstream news outlets got to cluck about the hippies invading the citadel, while high culture critics went out of the way to treat the composition and performance seriously. *New York Times* music critic Donal Henahan thought the opera "musically thin and otherwise rather ephemeral at times" but appreciated both the Who's "visceral punch" and the opera's "poignantly sentimental plot," which translated young people's generational trauma into "a tribal scream of togetherness."[3]

In *Rolling Stone*, Al Aronowitz delivers a delightfully churlish rejoinder, " 'Tommy' Does Not Vindicate Them."[4] Dismissing the booking at the Met as "just another gimmick," he sees the whole thing as a setup, a posturing, a "conditioned response, like Pavlov's dog." *Tommy* is not an opera, he asserts, it's incomprehensible, "the whole thing may as well be sung in Italian." Despite the occasional touching moments, "how can you take Daltrey seriously when he persists in fulfilling some 16-year-old's image of what a pop star should look like, with his frizzly hair and bare chest and idiot attempts at twirling the microphone on its cord, like a rookie cop still trying to learn how to swing his night stick?" And Pete? "Townshend may be an expert with pirouettes, entrechats and other dazzling leaps in his jump suit, but is that his music standing on its own feet? The Who is going to need more to vindicate itself than *Tommy*."[5]

Pete also was open to other manifestations and permutations of the opera, licensing rather freely for creative adaptations that sounded interesting to him, including a ballet. The 1971 performance and album with the London Symphony Orchestra further embedded the opera within a larger culture and testified to the composition's merit.

It seems inevitable that there would be a movie version. From the start, Pete and Kit had imagined a film, but I'm not sure if they imagined the film they got. The movie version of *Tommy* is absolutely bonkers, either an unforgiveable bastardization of Pete's vision or its brilliant realization, beyond even what Pete could ever come up with. Director Ken Russell is justly celebrated (or vilified) for "his gift for going too far, for creating three-ring cinematic circuses with kinky sideshows."[6] The film opens with Captain Walker's war, which is depicted by four women wearing lingerie, gas masks, and feathers in their hair traipsing through the burning, bomb-damaged landscape among the rescuers and firefighters. We know we are in for something special; whether it is to your taste or not is another question that need not derail us here.

Musically, the film does not hold up to the album or the live performances, not even the London Symphony Orchestra, which has some gorgeous orchestration of horns and strings if nothing else. Parts of the film sound like the lightweight, synthy TV cop-show soundtracks of the 1970s and 1980s; others are languid and flaccid (including the interminable, torpid Eric Clapton performance of "Eyesight to the Blind," which is only rescued when Arthur Brown jumps in to bring some fire to the proceedings).

Tina Turner and Elton John make the whole thing worthwhile in their performances—physically, musically, and vocally. Turner's Acid Queen devours the screen in carnal ferocity: erotic, rapacious, and terrifying. Playing the piano on his pinball machine with his ridiculously enormous "skyscraper" shoes, Elton's Pinball Wizard delivers what film critic Roger Ebert rightly calls "the movie's best single scene: a pulsating, orgiastic turn-on edited with the precision of a machine gun burst."[7] The piano works as well as Pete's power chords, and the buildup and denouement of the song work musically and visually. The Who get to recall their early career, appearing on-stage to smash their instruments, with the crowd carrying off Elton's boots. I believe the British would call the whole thing daft, but you wouldn't be crazy to think this version might be better than the original when Elton nails that high note "SURE plays a mean pinball."

Then there is Keith Moon's Uncle Ernie, which is all the more horrifying for its casual, almost Benny Hill characterization. The screen goes black as Uncle Ernie proceeds to "fiddle about," molesting Tommy, and Uncle Ernie returns with a corset on his head. It's definitely menacing, but a bit shocking to see how recognizable the character is from British comedic tradition—both salacious and silly.

While the cameos helped to market the film, the whole movie turns on Ann-Margret's performance as Tommy's mother: the core to the story as Russell delivers it. The very embodiment of the 1960s sex kitten, Ann-Margret is a force that bursts to the fullness of the screen, demanding our attention, first in her breakout performance in *Bye Bye Birdie* (1963) and especially in *Viva Las Vegas* (1964), where even Elvis almost—almost—has trouble keeping up. In fact, she's probably the only starlet who matches his power on-screen; while his is a cool and irresistible seduction, hers is all ravenous smiles and unceasing hips.

By the time of the *Tommy* movie, Ann-Margret is in her early thirties, an age when Hollywood was ready to send her out to pasture. She has calmed down a bit, at least at the start, so that we buy her as simply the young lover of Captain Walker during the "Overture," then the grieving mother trying to raise her boy who allows the predatory Oliver Reed to slide into her life. But her ferociousness awaits, unleashed when Walker returns and Oliver Reed kills him. This is the key change from the original album. Instead of the war hero Walker returning and killing the lover, an original sin and primal scene for Tommy, we have Oliver Reed, the deliciously sleazy, reptilian charmer, kill the father. So the family cannot be reunited under any circumstances. Ann-Margret joins Reed as sweaty, Fellini-esque grotesques, camera swooping in and out and across, the two of them chanting: "You didn't hear it, you didn't see it, you won't say nothing to no one, never tell a soul what you know is the truth." And again, Ann-Margret chants louder, more insistent, faster, more desperate, hair plastered across her face: "You didn't hear it, you didn't see it, you won't say nothing to no one, never tell a soul what you know is the truth." Cut to young Tommy's frozen face.

Now we go on Tommy's journey, but also his mother's. Perhaps Ann-Margret is a bit showbiz in her stylings for rock tastes of the 1970s, though I think she's brilliant in her sweaty desperation. She brings a fullness to the character of the mother in a way the album cannot. The album takes us through a series of potential cures, as Tommy is dragged by the mother to different doctors, but we see them as part of Tommy's story, and it's hard to flesh out the mother's motivation and sensibility. The movie highlights her story. She has to raise this child, to try to find a cure, all the while knowing that she did this to him. Her increasing desperation, leading to madness, derives not from the difficulty of being a mother to a deaf, dumb, and blind child, but from knowing what she has done. She is self-absorbed, unsympathetic, and pathetic, but Ann-Margret makes her character the center of the story. She descends into alcoholic decadence, and her outfits and hairstyles are worth the price alone. Meanwhile, Oliver Reed, as the lover, not the father, need only see Tommy as a problem to be solved, usually a distraction to be pushed aside, pawned off on whoever will take him. They are to some extent caricatures, but both actors relish their roles. And Ken Russell is clearly having fun, as the story builds and the scenes get more crazed.

The mother goes through escalating anguish coupled with attempts at desensitization, especially through the pursuit and display of wealth. Watching television, she sees a commercial for Rex Beans—"Fit for a Queen"—in a canny reference to *The Who Sell Out*. Ann-Margret is really in her element, with her jewels and champagne bottle, clad in a clinging, white jumpsuit, white furs trailing behind, in her all-white boudoir, and overcome by Tommy's image and silent pleas of "See Me Feel Me Touch Me Heal Me." No matter what she ingests, she cannot block it out; writhing on the bed, on the floor, champagne bottle in hand, she says, "I'd pay any price to drive his face from my thoughts."

Another commercial comes on the screen, alternating with the images in her mind of her son, this one for detergent.

She smashes the screen, and soap bubbles flood the room, with Ann-Margret writhing, sexily luxuriating, until baked beans flood out and she smears herself in them. Then brown sludge—I suppose it's supposed to be chocolate, but would viewers be wrong to think it looks like shit? She mounts a phallic pillow, straddling it, embracing it, rolling over and over.

Oh, and I forgot to mention that cherubic boy playing Tommy has been replaced by Roger Daltrey, stone-faced (except when Ann-Margret is stroking him) but still with flowing locks. Ann-Margret is only three years older than Daltrey. I'm no expert on Freud, but apparently Ken Russell is.

Now back in her boudoir, her red dress slit all the way up her thigh, singing in ecstasy and desperation, go-go dancing, swinging herself wildly, stroking the mirror with her writhing body, she gestures to smash the mirror with her champagne bottle, then climbs over Daltrey . . . "can you feel my temper rise, rise, rise." She throws Tommy through the mirror; he plummets and lands in a pool.

And that's it.

Tommy is cured.

But, wait. What just happened? Did Tommy's mother just seduce him? Yes. Yes, she did. Ann-Margret, with all her writhing—so much writhing—straddles Tommy and plunges him into adulthood.

The rest of the movie is a bit of a slog. The plot jumps into the merchandising of Tommy and the building of a cult. Tommy himself sure seems to be going along happily enough with the Tommy industry. The whole thing becomes slight, even silly, seemingly designed to show off shirtless Daltrey's prowess with swimming, cartwheels, and hang gliding. Tommy is still a cipher, acquiescent in the schemes and gladly playing the guru, but his motivation is suspect. The music is tame compared with the Who's originals, every song more flaccid, none of it as powerful as the album. "Sally Simpson" is reduced to a jaunty little ditty with goofy piano flourishes and claps. By the time we get to the rebellion of the followers in "We're Not Gonna Take It," even the guitar lead sounds meandering, not like Pete.

In the end, the followers kill Tommy's parents. He crawls to his dead and bloodied mother ("See me feel me touch me heal me") and walks out through the flaming, smashed pinball machines, dropping into the misty water ("listening to you, I get the music . . ."), swimming through the flow of the river, climbing out on the rocks, standing under the waterfall, climbing the mountain, all barefoot, shirtless, in jeans, arriving at the peak, overlooking lake and hills of the British countryside. We see him in silhouette against the rising sun as he lifts his arms slowly in salutation as the camera goes supernova. The final act feels desultory, still inscrutable, and, as the English would say, a damp squib.

Chapter 9

Tommy Reborn

Pete has been willing throughout his career to revisit *Tommy* and allow others to put their stamp on it. For a guy who seems totally controlling and uptight, he relishes the intervention of others. Pete joined forces with Des McAnuff to write and stage a musical version of *Tommy*. After a successful run in 1992 at the La Jolla Playhouse, *The Who's Tommy* opened on Broadway to tremendous success on April 22, 1993. Positive reviews, box office receipts, and Tony Awards all followed. By all accounts, the production was fantastic, fresh, original, and immersive, making brilliant use of screens and projections without sacrificing the humanity and grandeur of the actors and characters.

I am going to spend some time on the musical, possibly more than it deserves, probably more than you care to read. But stay with me, don't skip this. Because the play illuminates both a generation's reassessment of themselves and Pete's near-awareness of what the whole thing has always been about. *The Who's Tommy* reveals the tensions that have been at the heart of *Tommy* since Pete first wrote "Amazing Journey." Both the production and the responses illuminate the ways the trauma at the center of the story remains fundamentally unresolved.

Pete and Des made some key choices. They changed the timeline from WWI to WW2 so that the chronology makes sense, as now Tommy comes of age in the 1960s. The original chronology never made sense. They restored the story of the primal scene to its original, with the returning father killing the boyfriend. In the movie, Russell had flipped the story, so that Oliver Reed could play the depraved and unredeemable boyfriend. For the theater, Pete was insistent that the original story be restored, that we could only care about the family if the original unit was intact to suffer together, so that we could hope for their restoration. Pete even wrote a new song to fill in their desperation, making them, if not quite the heroes, sympathetic in their grieving.

This goes to a set of the deeper questions about every version of *Tommy*: how are we supposed to feel about the parents? The album seems to take them somewhat at face value: they are in pursuit of a cure for their ailing boy. But what drives them? Love for their son and parental devotion? Frustration and vanity, embarrassment at having such a son? Why do they abandon him at key moments, subjecting him first to their own abuse, then to his cousin's and uncle's, as well as to that of other charlatans and predators? How much does their own sense of guilt drive them? The play makes the family dynamic central for the first time.

Des came up with the two Tommys, with the five-year-old Tommy singing "See me, feel me, touch me, heal me" throughout the show, while the teen/adult Tommy evolves through the plot. The young Tommy never leaves, reflecting a new angle, that the loneliness and desperation of the child is universal and never leaves us. It's a nice touch, both making Tommy more universal and giving us a fuller picture of this individual. But that universality also erases the specifics of Tommy's treatment. And it leads us toward the most difficult-to-swallow part of the revised story: the uplifting ending.

Pete says that while rock thrives on open-endedness, the theater demands resolution. The theater experience needs the catharsis before the lights come up, and reviewers and audiences demand uplift. It's a simple matter of box-office reality: if you want audiences to flock to your Broadway theater, you had better promise them exaltation.

The show succeeds on that count. The whole show is a relentless rush of music and immersive staging, barely pausing for dialogue. The story makes a bit more sense, the characters are more fully realized, the performances stellar, the music calibrated to hold onto Pete's vision while adapting to the expectations of the audience. The staging is stunning, particularly when the whole auditorium is transformed into a pinball machine. The ending is rousing and sends the crowd out to the streets of New York, into the subways and taxis, off to dinner in the theater district, and back home to the surrounding suburbs in a state of rapture.

But is that what *Tommy* is about? Is that how we should really feel at the end of *Tommy*? Audiences loved the show. Reviews were generally favorable, though one musician in the show recalled that for "theater people it wasn't enough theater; for musical people, it was not enough musical; and rock people, it wasn't enough rock."[1] Guardians of the 1960s had mixed opinions.

The boomers were never more annoying than in the 1990s. Self-satisfied and self-centered, as always, they had emerged triumphant. While Reagan got too much credit for ending the Cold War, those who had come of age in the 1960s were now in charge. Bill Clinton, playing his saxophone, wanting to be Elvis, sat in the White House, and the end of history and the Dow 36,000 beckoned. The baby boom generation used the decade to settle scores with their elders, not by saying we told you so, but by honoring and co-opting them and basking in their glory by proxy. From Spielberg's *Saving Private Ryan* to Tom Brokaw's *The Greatest Generation*, the boomers skipped back over the 1960s to worship their parents' sacrifices and flood our pop culture with celebrations of what they were like before their kids came along. The boomers didn't need to apologize; they just got to elide their own lives and erase their own rejection of the parents' ethos. There was no score settling, really, just rewriting a celebratory and unifying history. No one mentioned that those very people who won the war on the streets of Europe and the sands of Iwo Jima then brought us Vietnam and Nixon. Like Joan Didion in 1967, in adulthood the counterculture was finally willing to embrace "the web" that "traditionally suggested and enforced society's values."[2]

Frank Rich (b. 1949), then the theater critic of the *New York Times*, later an op-ed columnist and cultural/political essayist, absolutely loved the show; he was completely unrestrained in his praise, calling it the first Broadway show to successfully capture the spirit of rock 'n' roll:

> "Tommy," the stunning new stage adaptation of the 1969 rock opera by the British group the Who, is at long last the authentic rock musical that has eluded Broadway for two generations. A collaboration of its original principal author, Pete Townshend, and the director, Des McAnuff, this show is not merely an entertainment juggernaut, riding at full tilt on the visual and musical highs of its legendary pinball iconography and irresistible tunes, but also a surprisingly moving resuscitation of the disturbing passions that made "Tommy" an emblem of its era.[3]

Rich praised the presentation of the "primal theme, expressed with devastating simplicity" of "the isolated young Tommy's totemic, recurring cry of yearning . . . [that] flows repeatedly between inner child and grown man, giving piercing voice to the eternal childhood psychic aches of loneliness and lovelessness." He lauded McAnuff and team: "they excavate the fable's meaning until finally the opera's revised conclusion spreads catharsis like wildfire through the cheering house."

The musical, he concluded, "reawaken[s] an audience's adolescent feelings of rebellion," but "takes a brave step further, concluding with a powerful tableau of reconciliation that lifts an audience of the 1990's out of its seats." Townshend, now in his forties, "hasn't got old so much as grown up, into a deeper view of humanity unthinkable in the late 1960's. Far from being another of Broadway's excursions into nostalgia, 'Tommy' is the first musical in years to feel completely alive in its own moment. No wonder that for two hours it makes the world seem young."[4]

Janet Maslin (b. 1949), the *Times'* film critic, similarly praises the show, claiming Pete and Des "have dusted off this rock-and-roll chestnut and coaxed forth a daring Broadway musical."[5] In a glowing portrait of McAnuff, Maslin claimed "this 'Tommy' exerts more visceral control over its audience than most Broadway musicals can" and credited the satisfying family reconciliation at the end to the creators' newfound maturity for these men in their forties: "Mr. McAnuff attributes some of its less messianic bent to the personal growth of Mr. Townshend, who had credited an 'avatar' for the original 'Tommy' album. 'I think his beliefs have evolved and changed,' said Mr. McAnuff. 'God, whose haven't?' " Only the less evolved would be so churlish as to hold on to a grudge against those parents.

The *Times'* music critic Jon Pareles (b. 1953) is not ready to play along. While conceding the show "has a thrilling score, eye-popping stage and visual effects, and a secure place in the memory of the baby-boomers every Broadway entrepreneur would love to draw," Pareles wants to make clear that this isn't "The Who's 'Tommy,' " as the title announces. Pete and Des have neutered the opera and betrayed the ghosts of Moon and Entwistle:

> Their changes turn a blast of spiritual yearning, con-
> fusion and rebellion into a pat on the head for nesters
> and couch potatoes.

As might be expected, Broadway's "Tommy" subdues most of the music, trading Roger Daltrey's rock belting for conventional Broadway emoting and taming the Who's glorious power chords with unnecessary keyboard doodling.[6]

In the *New Yorker*, theater critic John Lahr (b. 1941) similarly felt betrayed by the "marketing experience" that has replaced what was originally "one of the most splendid epitaphs" to the "brief bumptious moment of possibility" of the late 1960s. The new version brings us "adequate actors and dancers illustrating the words in prosaic Broadway-musical choreography . . . adroit without being inspired"—ouch—for "a middle-aged audience applauding the memory of youth." While "The Who were a fierce experience, not a suburban shuck," Broadway presents "the polyester version—shiny, easy to handle, and thin." With its rousing ending, "pandering to the masses is elevated to the level of metaphysics."[7]

One more, from *Rolling Stone*: Anthony DeCurtis (b. 1951) discovered what he most feared: "The Who's groundbreaking rock opera, a generational tale of erotic, hallucinogenic, and spiritual questing has been mainstreamed for the Nineties." Whereas the original *Tommy* was "a sprawling, confused, ambitious, and altogether compelling album that brilliantly captures the hopes, fears, urgency, and inarticulate fury of 1969, the tumultuous year of its release," the Broadway version presents a "nostalgic whiff of rebelliousness" capped off by "the play's revised, reassuring ending—extolling family values and social conformity" that "sends the audience home smiling and self-satisfied." DeCurtis honed in on the singing and musicianship, the technical proficiency that cannot capture the "yearning, cord-ravaging strain" of Daltrey's and Townshend's voices, and the poor drummer who cannot even try to capture "Moon's innate wildness, the vertiginous sense that he might take a song in any direction at any moment, just for the kicks."[8]

All these critics are baby boomers, born between 1941 and 1953, and even the theater critics retained a faith in the authenticity of rock that Broadway cannot capture. None of them is wrong. In fact, I love the passion of all the reviews. And there are many aspects of the play to admire. So much of the play seems brilliant and powerful. I especially loved Frank Rich's review, his joy at being able to give an unabashed, glowing review of a production that clearly meant a great deal to him, the play standing for so much more, for the whole 1960s journey in a way. I loved seeing him cherish a fresh appraisal of the era from a more mature, reflective perspective of the artist (and critic) now in their forties.

The musical allows all the characters to have their own perspectives, their own feelings and motivations, their own tragic backstories. Each actor has to come up with an interpretation that allows him or her to relate to, even cherish, the character. In the book released with the opening of the play, the actors' descriptions of their choices are fascinating and insightful.[9] Certain songs might even have been elevated in the production. On the album "Christmas" is a nice song, but small, closely observed, cut off from the larger world, a domestic curio, summarizing but not really adding to the larger story. It's almost another one of Pete's novelty songs, maybe not quite able to stand on its own. The play, by placing the scene in a majestic church setting, solemnizes and even raises the song. Changes made to songs such as "Acid Queen" and "Sally Simpson" also demonstrate the thoughtful evolution of the themes of *Tommy*; Pete is still developing the story in his own mind.

Only in creating this play does Pete claim to finally realize what *Tommy* is about. Pete accepts that the story is autobiographical, and even then, it seems that Pete identifies with the adolescent Tommy who faces the choice of accepting adulthood.[10] As he told an interviewer:

My work constantly readdresses a pivotal moment
around which I think most of our lives revolve in this
generation. I'm not sure about previous generations,
but I think if rock-and-roll is new, and if it's created
anything that's new and lasting, it's been the attention to the importance of that moment: the moment
when you are finally liberated from the protection of
family, community and society—at your own behest,
at your own demand. Suddenly, you are very, very
isolated, polarized and, most importantly, incredibly
alone, forever.[11]

What's changed now, in the 1990s, is that Pete sees that moment
of freedom as taking one back home. That means there's a whole
lot of reconciling going on.

The musical theater format demands that we identify with
the characters, and the production succeeds in this beautifully.
The parents, Uncle Ernie, and Cousin Kevin are fully developed,
carrying us through the whole story. They have to be likeable
enough, redeemable, and relatable. The play creates a group of
young toughs—"the lads"—as an evolving group, a sort of Greek
chorus, that in some ways represents our own connection to the
journey. But I struggle with all that. To me they seem like the
droogs in *A Clockwork Orange*, and I still wrestle with the parents,
who are presented as sympathetic, redeemable, maybe even heroic.

The parents bumble through a series of misguided attempts
to save Tommy, each more perverse and dangerous. I never
wanted to consider their motivations. But I'm with Tommy when
he smashes the mirror and then says screw you, I'm out (as the
play emphasizes). But even in the album, how does Uncle Ernie
get back into this? I get that he is a huckster, so he runs Tommy's
Holiday Camp. But what is Tommy thinking? What does Pete want
us to think? I still see the parents, the mother in particular, as

the villains, and Uncle Ernie and Cousin Kevin as evil predators. I want all those people to be condemned and shunned. Can we remember what the parents did in causing Tommy's suffering?

The musical asks us to see family reconciliation as the cathartic endpoint, and the beginning of the next stage of Tommy's story. Pete talks about how the format demands a tidy resolution, which is fine and understandable. He describes how rock songs and song cycles are allowed, even supposed, to leave things open, unresolved, a bit confusing. But a stage production needs the story to resolve. Fine. But it diminishes the story to a pat self-help formula. And when Tommy sings "I'm free," it's tough to take the new line: "And freedom lies here in normality."[12]

Could Pete and Des risk sending an audience home confused, frustrated, unsatisfied? Hell, no. They combine the rousing "We're Not Gonna Take It" with the comforting return to the warmth of home, bringing the characters back to each other where they started, finally allowing Tommy the home he was born into. But it's like Dorothy going back to Kansas, hardly fulfilling in the aftermath. Yes, we all click our heels together and incant "There's no place like home" . . . but then when we get home after the show, don't we regret just a bit that we have left the technicolor world behind? The play teaches us that release and relief come only as entertainment, in two-hour bites, dearly paid for. And we should not expect the world to be any different than it was two hours ago. We have no right to place any demands on the world other than the hope for the occasional respite. In fact, we are gonna take it. Tomorrow morning, after today's Sunday matinee, we will get up and go to work, expecting and accepting that things will be just the same. And our fucked-up families that abused us, well, we just have to accept them as they are, and our own place in the whole dynamic.

This seems to be the opposite of the rock 'n' roll promise. As Greil Marcus said about Elvis, what if rock'n'roll could be the whole thing, not just Saturday night, but all of life? And that certainly seems to be what Pete is after, especially in his spiritual pursuits—the complete integration of art and life. The whole discussion around the creation of play is delightful to read. At the beginning of the book that accompanies *The Who's Tommy*, he writes:

> Tommy is now on Broadway. People love it and people hate it, but I am in a new kind of ecstasy. This current interest in what was a naïve and impudent rock piece back in the late sixties has allowed me to reappraise my life as a writer. And I have learned that there is a vital difference between the simple rock song and the conventional musical theatre play—that it's necessary to bring a story to a conclusion, something you never have to do in rock-and-roll."[13]

From the first words he is embracing the joy of the new project and explaining what he sees as the greatest challenge for him (but also for his fans). Is he apologizing? Or is he embracing a new perspective on his role with glee: caring about what the people want? He seems completely at ease with what he did twenty-plus years earlier, but also with collaborating with Des McAnuff in reshaping it, allowing his creation to take new form, into a genre that he seems to have distrusted (maybe even disparaged) before.

Pete allows the ending to be more specific, and insists that the medium demands it. Is he selling out? Is he giving in too easily? Has he matured? Has he allowed the show to tarnish the original? Well, the original was hardly pure or perfect; I get the sense he relishes the whole production and is maybe talking himself into going along with what "the theatre" demands, but is also quite aware that he has extremely talented people around him who are collaborating on creating something truly extraordinary.

In the midst of all this, as he shares in his autobiography, Pete relapsed. Somewhere during the run-up to the opening on Broadway, Pete took his first drink in a decade and, as addicts are wont to do, kept drinking, getting sober again the following year. Pete may be a genius, but he is also a run-of-the-mill alcoholic and drug addict who has spent most of his adult years either using or trying not to use. He tried to quit when he first embraced Meher Baba in 1967. In the 1970s he was led to the NeuroElectric Therapy detoxification methods of Meg Patterson, which seemed to have worked for others. In 1984, he claimed to have been two years without a drink in a long conversation with Dennis Wholey, published in the book *The Courage to Change: Personal Conversations about Alcoholism.*[14]

I'm going to indulge in some cheap psychoanalysis—that the relapse had everything to do with the success of the musical and the submerged conflict that the show leaves unresolved, retreating even more than the original story did. The family reconciliation is premature. The trauma remains unhealed. It may also not be a coincidence that Pete was releasing a new solo record at the time, *Psychoderelict*, a concept album that hints at his own career trajectory and potential attraction to underage girls. The new solo production cries out for attention to the darkness still within, while the resolution in *The Who's Tommy* suppresses that darkness to wide acclaim. The musical is nominated for all sorts of awards, as if the world craves and rewards the happy ending. The critics—his generational peers—also want the story resolved and closed. Those who loved the musical were no doubt heartfelt—and they weren't necessarily wrong—but the catharsis comes from finally bringing a closure to the trauma, a satisfactory conclusion that allows them to move on. The relapse comes from the avoidance of the deeper wound, once again.

This is all speculative, maybe unfair. And there's a further paradox that during this period Pete sounds completely at ease, filled with wisdom and acceptance about the story itself and the whole process. In interviews and his own accounts in the book that is released with the show, Pete seems to have found a new peace, and his perspective is suffused with the language of recovery. It looks like sober living, sober thinking, sober spirituality, even if not with full commitment. Pete emphasizes that the whole purpose of life is to submit. This is a Meher Baba philosophy, but it is also the language of the twelve-step program of Alcoholics Anonymous, whose first step is "We admitted we were powerless over alcohol—that our lives had become unmanageable." We have to admit complete defeat and "turn our lives and our will over to the care of god as we understand him."

To get started in this program, they tell us, we have to have "hit bottom," and we have to have come to the point of giving up completely—I cannot do this myself; all the plans, formulas, schemes I have devised to control my drinking (and drug use) and manage my life have failed. I surrender absolutely. Go ahead and hold onto a shortcut, a clever plan, an asterisk, and you will not stay sober for long. Until you have accepted completely that you cannot do it yourself, you will not be able to create a foundation. Alcoholics are "childish, emotionally sensitive, and grandiose." The program describes the disease of alcoholism in the harshest of terms—a "rampaging juggernaut" and "rapacious creditor" that takes us to "our bankruptcy as going human concerns" and "absolute humiliation" and, if we are lucky, "utter defeat" that allows us to "take our first steps toward liberation and strength." From this moment of liberation can come a life of recovery.

It all starts with admitting complete defeat and accepting (finding) a higher power to guide your life. Pete had been following a higher power since discovering Meher Baba more than twenty years earlier. The submission in the original *Tommy* is confusing. When his mother smashes the mirror, what, exactly, happens to Tommy? What is he doing? He is taking agency? Is that an act of self-will or of submission to a higher power, of acceptance of one's fate and purpose? Is smashing the mirror breaking "the bondage of self," as AA literature puts it? The original album is a bit inscrutable, as many have noted, but the songs redeem any shortcomings. The musical is actually formally better in terms of plot, character development, narrative resolution. All of the characters are real characters. The story is really a family story, one that allows each of the family members to have their own motivation, dramatic arc, and some sympathy from the audience. But the message shifts. And the musical takes us right back into the belly of the abusers. Even in the original it is sketchy that Uncle Ernie never goes away, but on the stage Uncle Ernie and Cousin Kevin are major players throughout the story. Gone is the child Tommy, despite the fact that he returns throughout the performance. It's now about the teenager coming of age who must accept that his parents are flawed, but human. He must reconcile to the reality around him. The ending of the musical is exactly the sort of "spiritual shortcut" that Pete has railed against for twenty-five-plus years, exactly the refusal to confront what AA literature calls the "the great reality within."

Conclusion

To the *Lifehouse*

Pete wants desperately for there to be no pain. He aches for the one note that will contain everything, the pure and evil, heaven and hell, all of human experience, resonating into one musical vibration. He wants that one note to be all of life. The *Lifehouse* project that was to follow *Tommy* (but was never realized in its original version) imagined people inhabiting a rock show for perhaps six months at a time. Pete references the Grateful Dead experience as perhaps the closest thing to what he was trying to do. How can we create an immersive rock experience that is NOT simply an escape, but launches a transformation, becomes itself the whole of life?

After tinkering with *Lifehouse*, Pete had to abandon it for a couple decades. Many of the songs were gathered for the band's next studio album, *Who's Next*, generally and probably justifiably considered their best. "Baba O'Riley" can lay claim to being their best song. Or maybe "Won't Get Fooled Again," which I want to focus on here, as fulfilling one path of Pete's trajectory of seeking.

"Won't Get Fooled Again" strikes me as deeply cynical in the guise of wise. Whatever the original intent, the song serves—in its catchphrases—as a slogan for the passive and accepting of all as it is. The lyrics become rants that seem to offer wisdom, but encourage passivity. "Meet the new boss, same as the old boss" seems to say: I won't be fooled by the optimism of the 1960s, by those who claimed we can make a better world, because change is not possible.[1]

If "We're Not Gonna Take It" was a rejection of authority, an anti-fascist song[2] even, "Won't Get Fooled Again" tells us not to bother, giving the whole audience, the whole generation, an out, an excuse to no longer follow anyone—be it JFK or the Yippies—and thus retreat into self-help and domesticity, smugly invoking their wisdom in seeing through, embracing a cynicism so that the song becomes an anthem of self-satisfied, conservative domesticity. We sing along and wait for Daltrey's glorious scream to exorcise any hope for social transformation.

On the other path of Pete's spiritual journey comes "Pure and Easy," which also emerged from these sessions, but did not make it onto *Who's Next*. Too bad. The song did not make the cut but was what gave *Lifehouse* "the whole concept its governing principle."[3] It saw vinyl on Pete's first solo album (the later Who version was released on *Odds and Sods*, a collection of random songs). It really captures Pete's pursuit, and it is deeply persona and spiritual, not social. He talks continually during this period about wanting to find the Universal note or chord, the one sound that will harmonize all of humanity with the universe. He references the vibrations that come at moments of performing.

"There once was a note, pure and easy . . ." This is what Pete is searching for, or moving toward at all times, finding himself pulled in that direction, with all of his obstacles. That is his story. How do I get to that universal note, what Sufi teacher Inayat Khan calls the Lost Chord. For Pete, when that moment comes, listeners will "actually leave their bodies" like he did in the air over the Atlantic in 1967.[4] As Dave Marsh sees it, " 'Pure and Easy' is an even more profoundly moving portrait of the constant hope that that possibility will be achieved, of the acceptance of life's horror, of coming to terms with human frailty without wallowing in blame or guilt. It is Peter Townsend's greatest statement of his beliefs; it is perhaps rock's greatest song of faith."[5]

"Pure and Easy" is my favorite Pete song, his voice lovely, singing, "There once was a note pure and easy / Playing so free like a breath rippling by," the guitar ringing sweetly. All of Pete's themes are in there. The grappling with how to convey everything in one song. In one note, really. The note is in us. It is out there—"The note is eternal / I hear it, it sees me / Forever we blend as forever we die"—making everything, destroying everything. It includes a million people cheering and a child angel riding in a star. Death and destruction are pure and easy as well. It's all a simple secret. The note in us all. The transformation must be personal, not social.

Postscript

What Happened to Pete

On January 4, 2003, Pete was arrested for possession of child pornography. Ultimately no evidence of downloaded images was found and charges were not filed, but he did not contest the decision to place him on the British sex offenders list. His claim that he was investigating the complicity of banks in laundering money for pedophile rings is plausible enough. Can I accept Pete's version? Sure, why not? As a historian, I often have to accept the evidence that is there, accept as a provisional truth what is known, always ready to revise upon presentation of new evidence or interpretation. Do I think we know everything about the JFK assassination? Sure. Would I be surprised if more were to be revealed? Hell, no.

Pete says he was doing research to expose the online child porn world. As a near-megalomaniacal artist, he would certainly be capable of doing that, going off on his own without collaborators or even an alibi. But would I be surprised if a man who was sexually abused and who had lived a life of compulsion was drawn to child porn? Sadly, no. And Pete has specifically mentioned how his memories are incomplete, but the sexualized or erotic connection is there. That's all he knows.

In 2012, Pete released his autobiography, *Who I Am*. He reveals that his grandmother abused him during a traumatic year he spent living with her. The autobiography maturely assesses the realistic factors and explains convincingly what happened. But the child only knows that the parents are not to be trusted. Then the grandmother, the madwoman, has her way, because she knows no limits, accepts no boundaries, in her mental illness cocoon has concocted a scheme where she is not responsible for what she does; she is not well after all, so she may do as she pleases.

Pete needs Tommy to suffer so that he does not have to. Tommy shuts down, so Pete can keep going. How does Pete not shut down? What did his grandmother do to him? What did she SAY to him? Dare I wonder if others abused him, if he had an Uncle Ernie and Cousin Kevin?

Pete: "And my experience of abuse as a child is something which I don't fully recall. I get the sense that there is something that has happened to me as a child, something that is erotic or sexual or disturbing or dark or something in nature, because of dreams that I've had and memories that I have. But I was very, very young, y'know I was between the ages of four and five and a half and when I was with my grandmother and I just know that some weird shit went down."[1]

Did she also tell him, "You didn't hear it, you didn't see it, you won't say nothing to no one, never tell a soul what you know is the truth"? In fact, those words never really need to be said to the abused. It is understood. After all, his parents are the ones who were so absorbed in their own lives that they abandoned him to his crazy grandmother's care for a year. He knows they do not want to hear what has been happening to him while they were attending to their own desires.

So I have to accept that the authorities decided not to prosecute Pete (though he was placed on the sex offenders list), and in the absence of evidence refuting his version, I will take it. I hesitate to hail him as a hero for confronting what others of us would never dream of doing because I might be wrong. But it fits within the fearless and challenging Pete we have lived with all these years.

He proceeds to share his story with his fans. He writes his autobiography, tells his story, concluding with a sweet, tender, healing letter to his eight-year-old self ("Today you are adorable, a lovely boy").[2] He does the requisite public explication and publicity tour. And, then, no more.

This is why Tommy must only see the action in the mirror—Pete cannot look at it directly. A Lacanian psychoanalytic reading of the "mirror stage" tells us that during the traumatic scene, Tommy's "self-image—which had originally been positive and coherent—breaks down," and he "blocks himself out" and "paradoxically chooses to disappear in order to continue to be loved."[3] That is why Pete cannot see the story of Tommy as autobiographical, cannot fully identify with the child Tommy, must keep him external. And this is why Pete must continually offer premature forgiveness. From the insistence in "A Quick One" that "you are forgiven," to the original conception of Tommy as a blank slate, to the musical's restoration and rehabilitation of the family, he's always wanted to find a shortcut to forgiveness in order to forgive himself.

In the last generation or so, there has been a great deal of attention to the effects of trauma, led by the work of Judith Herman and Peter Levine and therapies based on somatic experiencing, parts therapy, polyvagal theory, and others. Researchers and therapists have explored the connections between childhood sexual assault, trauma, and addiction, making it clear that healing can be a lifetime's work.

I find the shortcuts frustrating, offering absolution to those who don't deserve it. But I cannot blame Pete for rejecting my query. He has done what he can do—multiple times throughout his life, first creating *Tommy*, then revisiting and revising, opening himself up in so many ways, collaborating, trusting, talking, talking, talking—confronting and avoiding his trauma again and again. He is entitled, after giving us—giving me—so much, to close the book on this story, to say to me, "I want nothing to do with it."

Notes

Chapter 3

1. Casey Harrison, *Feedback: The Who and Their Generation* (Lanham, MD: Rowman & Littlefield, 2015), 34. Actually, Pete was born on May 19, and it appears Speer was captured on May 15 and formally arrested on May 23, 1945.

2. Jann S. Wenner, "Pete Townshend Talks Mods, Recording, and Smashing Guitars, *Rolling Stone*, September 14, 1968.

3. Winston Churchill, Speech to the House of Commons, June 18, 1940, and Speech to the House of Commons, June 4, 1940, https://winston-churchill.org/resources/speeches/1940-the-finest-hour/their-finest-hour/ and https://winstonchurchill.org/resources/speeches/1940-the-finest-hour/we-shall-fight-on-the-beaches/.

4. Winston Churchill, Speech to the House of Commons, June 4, 1940.

5. Pete Townshend, *Who I Am* (New York: HarperCollins, 2012), 340.

6. Harrison, *Feedback*, 31.

7. Jann S. Wenner, "Pete Townshend Settles Down," *Rolling Stone*, September 28, 1968, 18.

8. "It was based on the rise of an economic, political, and increasingly Anglophone North Atlantic that offered ample opportunity for pop music to appeal across wide social and geographic boundaries." Harrison, *Feedback*, 59.

9. Pete Townshend, *Who I Am*, 340.

10. Wenner, "Pete Townshend Talks Mods."

11. Wenner, "Pete Townshend Talks Mods."

12. Wenner, "Pete Townshend Talks Mods."
13. Wenner, "Pete Townshend Talks Mods."
14. Wenner, "Pete Townshend Talks Mods."
15. Quoting from Johnny Black, *Eyewitness: The Who* (London: Carlton Publishing Group, 2001), 47; Harrison, *Feedback*, 36.
16. Quoting Pete from *Quadrophenia: Director's Cut*, "Two Stormy Summers," 17; Harrison, *Feedback*, 108–9.
17. Charles Perry and Andrew Bailey, "The Who's Spooky Tour: Awe and Hassles," *Rolling Stone*, January 3, 1974. Quoted in Dave Marsh, *Before I Get Old: The Story of the Who* (1983; repr., London: Plexus, 2015), 118.
18. Greil Marcus, "Interview with Pete Townshend," *Rolling Stone*, June 26, 1980.
19. Marsh, *Before I Get Old*, 168.
20. On "My Generation" and especially the stutter, see Marsh, *Before I Get Old*, 156–57. It was mostly about a mod being on pills, says Marsh citing Roger.
21. Marsh, *Before I Get Old*, 160.
22. Quoting from Geoffrey Giuliano, *Behind Blue Eyes: The Life of Pete Townshend* (New York: Cooper Square Press, 2002), 64–65; Harrison, *Feedback*, 100.
23. Gustav Metzger, "Auto-Destructive Art Manifesto." Second Manifesto, London, March 10, 1960.
24. Michael Zwerin, "Jazz Journal—Bird Who," *Village Voice*, April 11, 1968. See also Marsh, *Before I Get Old*, 51–52, 112–13; Mark Brown, "Gustav Metzger, Pioneer of Auto-destructive art, Dies Aged 90," *The Guardian*, March 1, 2017, https://www.theguardian.com/education/2017/mar/02/auto-destructive-art-pioneer-gustav-metzger-dies-aged-90.

Chapter 4

1. Joan Didion, "Slouching Towards Bethlehem," in Didion, *Slouching Towards Bethlehem* (New York: Farrar, Straus and Giroux, 2017), 179–80; originally published in *Saturday Evening Post*, September 27, 1967.
2. For an interesting take on Didion and the article, see Louis Menand, "Out of Bethlehem: The Radicalization of Joan Didion," *New Yorker*, August 24, 2015, https://www.newyorker.com/magazine/

2015/08/24/out-of-bethlehem. And for a review that assesses Didion's remarks ("Let me tell you, it was gold") about the scene that ends the essay, see Rebecca Mead, "The Most Revealing Moment in the New Joan Didion Documentary," *New Yorker*, October 27, 2017, https://www.newyorker.com/culture/cultural-comment/the-most-revealing-moment-in-the-new-joan-didion-documentary.

    3. Mat Snow, *The Who: 50 Years of My Generation* (New York: Race Point Publishing, 2015), 58.

    4. The Who, *Live at Leeds*, 1995 CD reissue, Polydor.

    5. Pete Townshend, *Who I Am* (New York: HarperCollins, 2012), 101.

    6. Richard Barnes and Pete Townshend, *The Story of Tommy* (Twickenham: Eel Pie Publishing, 1977), 11.

    7. Barnes and Townshend, *The Story of Tommy*, 18.

    8. Certain parts of "Rael pts. 1 & 2" return on *Tommy* in "Underture" and "Sparks."

    9. Dave Marsh, *Before I Get Old: The Story of the Who* (1983, repr., London: Plexus, 2015;), 227.

    10. Casey Harrison, *Feedback: The Who and Their Generation* (Lanham, MD: Rowman & Littlefield, 2015), 132.

    11. Chris Welch, "Who Needs to Take Pop Seriously," *Melody Maker*, December 30, 1967.

    12. See Mark Blake, *Pretend You're in a War: The Who and the Sixties* (London: Aurum Press, 2014; and "Pete Townshend vs Jimi Hendrix: The Who Backstage at Monterey," *Mojo4music*, September 4, 2015, mojo4music.com/articles/21631/pete-townshend-vs-jimi-hendrix-the-who-backstage-at-monterey.

    13. Robert Christgau, "Anatomy of a Love Festival," *Esquire*, January 1968, 152.

    14. Mike Daly, *Mojo Navigator R&R News* 2, no. 2 (August 1967), http://deadsources.blogspot.com/2012/02/june-18-1967-monterey-pop-festival.html.

    15. Michael Lydon, "Monterey Pop: The First Rock Festival," September 22, 2009, https://www.criterion.com/current/posts/231-monterey-pop-the-first-rock-festival; originally written in 1967 and included in the Criterion Collection's 2002 edition of *Monterey Pop*.

    16. Quoted in Joe Livernois, "The Dead's Redemption at Monterey, and the Filming of 'Touch of Grey,'" September 11, 2019, https://voicesofmontereybay.org/2019/09/11/monterey-rocks-19/.

17. Quoted in Emma Silvers, "Phil Lesh: Grateful Dead 'Didn't Deliver' at First Monterey Pop," *Rolling Stone*, June 23, 2017, https://www.rollingstone.com/music/music-features/phil-lesh-grateful-dead-didnt-deliver-at-first-monterey-pop-200717/.

18. Robert Christgau, "Anatomy of a Love Festival," *Esquire*, January 1968, 152. He originally wrote "psychedelic Uncle Tom," but *Esquire* rejected that language. See http://www.robertchristgau.com/xg/music/monterey-69.php.

Chapter 5

1. John Tobler and Conner McKnight, "Chatting with Pete Townshend," *ZigZag* #24, October 1971.

2. Pete Hamill, "Rock of Ages," *New York*, October 18, 1982, 41.

3. Martin R. Smith, dir., *The Who: The Making of Tommy* (Eagle Rock Productions and BBC Four Video, 2013).

4. Pete Townshend, "In Love with Meher Baba," *Rolling Stone* #71, November 26, 1970, https://www.rollingstone.com/music/music-news/in-love-with-meher-baba-by-pete-townshend-237859/.

5. Chris Charlesworth and Mike McInnerney, *Tommy at 50: The Mood, the Music, the Look, and the Legacy of The Who's Legendary Rock Opera* (New York: Apollo Publishers, 2019), 28. This recent publication is a delightful and insightful addition to the growing shelf of books about the Who.

6. Townshend, "In Love with Meher Baba."

7. Townshend, "In Love with Meher Baba."

8. Townshend, "In Love with Meher Baba."

9. Townshend, "In Love with Meher Baba."

10. Townshend, "In Love with Meher Baba."

Chapter 6

1. Meher Baba quoted in Cameron Crowe, "Pete Townshend Penthouse Interview," *Penthouse*, December 1974, 96.

2. Casey Harrison, *Feedback: The Who and Their Generation* (Lanham, MD: Rowman & Littlefield, 2015), 61.

3. See the fantastic articles and interviews in Mark Sinker, ed., *A Hidden Landscape Once a Week* (London: Strange Attractor Press, 2018), especially Jon Savage, "Dangerous, Paul," 72–85.

4. Dave Marsh, *Before I Get Old: The Story of the Who* (1983; repr., London: Plexus, 2015), 106.

5. Harrison, *Feedback*, 62–63.

6. Chris Welch, "Who Needs to Take Pop Seriously," *Melody Maker*, December 30, 1967.

7. Don Paulsen, "Pete Townshend Discusses The Live Who," *Hit Parader*, February 1968.

8. Keith Altham, "Pete Townshend Keeps The Who Live," *New Music Express*, November 16, 1968.

9. From interview with Cameron Crowe in *Penthouse*, December 1974; quoted in Marsh, *Before I Get Old*, 125.

10. Quoted in Marsh, *Before I Get Old*, 297.

11. From interview with Cameron Crowe in *Penthouse*, December 1974; quoted in Marsh, *Before I Get Old*, 126.

12. *Quadrophenia: Director's Cut*, "Two Stormy Summers"; quoted in Harrison, *Feedback*, 62–63.

13. "I don't like fans really. But that's because they're my employer—I don't like the boss." In Simon Garfield, "Won't Get Fooled Again," *Intelligent Life Magazine* (Summer 2011), https://www.igtc.com/pipermail/thewho/2011-May/022628.html, https://www.simongarfield.com/pete-townshend-who-he-is/, and https://www.economist.com/prospero/2011/05/27/whats-pete-townshend-up-to-these-days.

14. Richard Barnes and Pete Townshend, *The Story of Tommy* (Twickenham: Eel Pie Publishing, 1977), 30.

15. Pete gave different accounts of this interview, especially regarding what substances were ingested. In one recounting, he recalls asking Wenner if he had dosed him with acid. In his autobiography, he refers to the presence of cocaine at Casady's house, but does not acknowledge his own use. But in another interview with *Rolling Stone* in 1970, Pete says, "I was very hyped up on coke." See Townshend, *Who I Am* (New York: HarperCollins, 2012), 148–49; and Jonathan Cott, "A Talk with Pete Townshend," *Rolling Stone* 58, May 14, 1970, 35.

16. In the final version, it is not the father who beats Tommy, but Cousin Kevin who tortures him.

17. Townshend, *Who I Am*, 17.

18. Nik Cohn, "'Tommy,' The Who's Pinball Opera," *New York Times*, May 18, 1969, page ARTS36 of the New York edition. In later years both Pete and Nik told various half-serious versions of a story claiming an exchange of this song for a positive review from Cohn.

19. Albert Goldman, "A Grand Opera in Rock," *Life*, October 17, 1969, 20.

20. Albert Goldman, " 'Tommy': The Red Dawn of Revolt?," *New York Times*, November 30, 1969, D30.

Chapter 7

1. From interview with Cameron Crowe in *Penthouse*, December 1974; quoted in Dave Marsh, *Before I Get Old: The Story of the Who* (1983; repr., London: Plexus, 2015), 126.

2. Audio of the incident is available at https://www.youtube.com/watch?v=Q8BYgzIEHIY&t=78s.

3. Marsh, *Before I Get Old*, 288.

4. Marsh, *Before I Get Old*, 288.

5. Jonathan Cott, "Pete Townshend Interview," *Rolling Stone* #58, May 14, 1970.

6. Peter Doggett, *There's a Riot Going On: Revolutionaries, Rock Stars, and the Rise and Fall of the 60s* (New York: Canongate Books, 2007), 267–77.

7. Mat Snow, *The Who: 50 Years of My Generation* (New York: Race Point Publishing, 2015), 94. It was not still live. He unplugged it. You can see on the film.

8. Henry Diltz, Interview with John Beaudin on *RockhistoryMusic.com*, https://www.youtube.com/watch?v=53c6TnJG_fA. And Henry Diltz, *Vol. 3: Woodstock*, https://vimeo.com/352798774.

9. See Cott, "Pete Townshend Interview." Hoffman attempted his revenge with *Woodstock Nation* (New York: Random House, 1969), where he prints a mock version of "We're Not Gonna Take It," including lines like, "The money is the message Who?"

10. Marsh, *Before I Get Old*, 284.

11. Townshend quoted in Marsh, *Before I Get Old*, 344.

12. Marsh, *Before I Get Old*, 354.

13. Marsh, *Before I Get Old*, 384.

14. Marsh, *Before I Get Old*, 161.

15. Rick Sanders and David Dalton, "Pete and Tommy Among Others," *Rolling Stone* #37, July 12, 1969.

16. Richard Barnes and Pete Townshend, *The Story of Tommy* (Twickenham: Eel Pie Publishing, 1977), 31.

17. Steve Peacock, "Pete Townshend—Rock Music in the Future," *Sounds*, July 27, 1971.

Chapter 8

1. Nik Cohn, "Finally, the Full Force of The Who," *New York Times*, March 8, 1970, M2.

2. Cohn, "Finally, the Full Force of The Who," M2.

3. Donal Henahan, " 'Tommy' Is Poignantly Sentimental," *New York Times*, June 8, 1970, 42.

4. Alfred G. Aronowitz, " 'Tommy' Does Not Vindicate Them," *Rolling Stone*, July 9, 1970, 18.

5. Aronowitz, " 'Tommy' Does Not Vindicate Them."

6. Roger Ebert, "Tommy," January 1, 1975, https://www.rogerebert. com/reviews/tommy-1975.

7. Roger Ebert, "Tommy."

Chapter 9

1. Quoted in Elizabeth L. Wollman, *The Theater Will Rock: A History of the Rock Musical, from Hair to Hedwig* (Ann Arbor: University of Michigan Press, 2006), 170. Wollman has an overview of the musical's reception. She also claims, "Part of the problem lay in the fact that in attempting to appeal to rock and theater camps alike, *The Who's Tommy* alienated both" in *Bad Music: The Music We Love to Hate*, ed. Christopher Washburne, Christopher J. Washburne, and Maiken Derno (New York: Routledge, 2004), 315.

2. Joan Didion, "Slouching Towards Bethlehem," in Didion, *Slouching Towards Bethlehem* (New York: Farrar, Straus and Giroux, 2017), 179–80; orig. published in *Saturday Evening Post*, September 27, 1967.

3. Frank Rich, "Review/Theater: Tommy; Capturing Rock-and-Roll and the Passions of 1969," *New York Times*, April 23, 1993.

4. Rich, "Review/Theater: Tommy; Capturing Rock-and-Roll and the Passions of 1969."

5. Janet Maslin, "The Man Who Reinvented the Who's 'Tommy,'" *New York Times*, May 9, 1993.

6. Jon Pareles, "Critic's Notebook; Damping 60's Fire of 'Tommy' for 90's Broadway," *New York Times*, April 27, 1993.

7. John Lahr, "Full Tilt," *The New Yorker*, May 3, 1993, 96–98.

8. Anthony DeCurtis, "Opinion: Broadway Production of *Tommy*," *Rolling Stone*, June 24, 1993 (rpt. in DeCurtis, *Rocking My Life Away: Writing about Music and Other Matters*, [Durham, NC: Duke University Press, 1998], 253–54).

9. Pete Townshend, *The Who's Tommy: The Musical* (New York: Pantheon Books, 1993).

10. Jon Pareles, "THEATER; 'Tommy' and His Father Reach Broadway," *New York Times*, March 28, 1993.

11. "Townshend Lets Loose," Interview by Rita D. Jacobs, in Pete Townshend, *The Who's Tommy: The Musical* (New York: Pantheon Books, 1993), 84.

12. Which Pete excuses as a "lazy rhyme." Anthony DeCurtis, "Pete Townshend, Opera Man," *Rolling Stone*, December 23, 1993, https://www.rollingstone.com/music/music-news/pete-townshend-opera-man-97582/.

13. Des McAnuff and Pete Townshend, *The Who's Tommy: The Musical*, 1993

14. Dennis Wholey, *The Courage to Change: Personal Conversations about Alcoholism* (Boston: Warner Books, 1984).

Conclusion

1. As Pete told *Rolling Stone* in 2016, in perhaps one of his surlier moods, " 'Won't Get Fooled Again' is an anti-revolution song and I don't think there's been a revolution worth the paper it's been written on. Ever. But maybe I haven't read enough history to get that right. I don't know that I would indict anybody who would want to revolt against the establishment today, but it's interesting. I did it and I said it then and I stood by it and I can stand by it today." Kory Grow, "Pete Townshend Talks 'Quieter' 'Tommy' Concert, the Who's Future," *Rolling Stone*, December 2, 2016, https://www.rollingstone.com/music/music-features/pete-townshend-talks-quieter-tommy-concert-the-whos-future-110127/.

2. Richard Barnes and Pete Townshend, *The Story of Tommy* (Twickenham: Eel Pie Publishing, 1977), 114.

3. Mat Snow, *The Who: 50 Years of My Generation* (New York: Race Point Publishing, 2015), 109.

4. Dave Marsh, *Before I Get Old: The Story of the Who* (1983; repr., London: Plexus, 2015), 304.

5. Marsh, *Before I Get Old*, 314.

Index